BRAVE GREATNESS

The Driven Woman's Guide to NOT Having It All

Charlie McClain

Brave Greatness
Las Vegas, Nevada

For permission requests, email assistant@writercharliemcclain.com
Brave Greatness | McClain Empowerment Group, LLC.
writercharliemcclain.com
Brave Greatness/Charlie McClain – 1st ed.
ISBN 979-8-9918632-1-6

— ♥ —

To

Anna

Nicholas

and Riff Raff.

Thank you for being in my soul cluster.

I love you.

CONTENTS

Introduction

The Liberation of NOT Having It All

My friends often tell me I've lived enough for several lifetimes, and perhaps they're right. I've navigated the chaotic aisles of grocery stores with a four-year-old in my cart, a toddler in one arm, and a shopping list in the other, somehow balanced work deadlines with school pickups—all while trying to be the perfect mother, partner, employee—you name it. Like many women, I bought into the myth that I could—and should—have it all. If I just tried hard enough, juggled a little faster, and slept a little less, I could meet the relentless demands without dropping a single ball.

I've survived abuse, become an expert on narcissistic behaviors, rode a motorcycle for five years, started and closed several businesses, and experienced homelessness on at least two different occasions. I know what it is to be rich, poor, and everything in between. Through all of these things, I raised two kids. When my son was in his early and mid-twenties, I walked alongside him through the challenges of schizoaffective disorder. He is lost to me now, and in my heart of hearts, I believe he is probably deceased. But without proof, the journey of mourning him never fully begins or ends.

So, here I am talking to you about Brave Greatness and the liberation of *not* having it all. I will be vulnerable here and share with you that there are times when I have faltered in writing this book. There have been so many moments when my subconscious threw every excuse at me for why I should *not* act like some expert trying to tell anyone anything at all.

And yet… I was born to share this information. I believe that in my heart, and so here I am, sharing with you *not* how to be like me but rather how I learned that while the most challenging thing we can do is completely embrace being ourselves, it is possible. I'm here to share my journey toward that incredibly difficult objective, toward *not* having it all, in hopes that some woman like me out there benefits from it.

To be honest, striving to have it all nearly broke me. The constant hustle, endless lists, and unspoken expectations were exhausting. And I know I'm not alone in this.

Like so many, I've spent a lifetime reading self-improvement books. As a professional coach, I've come to believe we've all been sold this rather fragmented approach to self-improvement. As coaches, we are told we must focus on one niche and specialize. As clients, we are told to fix one part of ourselves at a time—as if our lives were neatly divided into separate compartments—or as if we can hire fifteen coaches to help us. But the truth is, there is no disconnect. All of 'the work' is the work—all of it intertwined, messy, and beautifully complex. With that in mind, know that this book is written to cover *some* of the work, as no one book can possibly cover it all.

This isn't the part where I tell you how I figured it all out—because I didn't. What I have discovered is that the pursuit of having it all is a surefire way to lose ourselves. It's a chase that leaves us exhausted, overcommitted, and disconnected from our true desires.

It's time for a new paradigm. What if embracing our limitations is the path to true greatness? What if letting go of the impossible standards we've internalized allows us to focus on what genuinely brings us joy and peace?

My journey toward allowing—allowing myself to rest, to say no, to be imperfect—began when I least expected it. It wasn't a grand epiphany but a series of small moments that forced me to confront the unsustainable pace I'd set for myself. Fifteen years of abusive relationships and five years of doing what we now call 'the work' allowed me to finally begin to recognize the pressures of having it all for what they are: a societal construct designed to keep us perpetually striving and never arriving.

I realized I was suffering under the weight of society's expectations and my own. I was caught in the triple trap of pleasing, performing, and perfecting—a phenomenon I call Driven Woman Syndrome. I was so busy trying to be everything to everyone that I lost sight of who I was.

Ten years later, here we are. This book, Brave Greatness, is about that journey and the liberation that comes from *not* having it all. It's about rejecting the fragmented approach to self-improvement and embracing the whole, imperfect, wonderful mess that we are. It's about understanding that balance is a myth and that peace—*true, deep, inner peace*—is what we're really seeking.

We'll explore the energetics of overcommitment, the invisible weight of expectations, and the cost of striving for an unattainable ideal. We'll delve into recognizing unacknowledged trauma and how allowing those parts of ourselves out of the closet—but not into the arena—can lead to healing. But more importantly, we'll journey together toward redefining success on our own terms, cultivating self-compassion, and embracing Brave Greatness.

I'm not here to offer a magic pill or a step-by-step guide to perfection. Instead, I'm inviting you to sit with me in the stillness, to ask yourself, "What *don't* I want?" Sometimes it's easier to start there. By identifying what no longer serves us, we make room for what truly brings us joy and fulfillment.

So, if you're tired of the juggling act, of the relentless pursuit of an impossible ideal, this book is for you. Let's embark on this journey together—a sisterhood of dynamic women ready to become unapologetic, visionary leaders of our own lives. Let's find the peace that's been waiting for us all along.

Part I:

Understanding Driven Woman Syndrome

Chapter 1

The Triple Trap—Pleasing, Performing, Perfecting

Throughout this book, I will mention some of the challenges I've faced in my life thus far. Some of these challenges relate to abuse, both as a child and an adult. I won't swim around in it or provide gory details. It may even come across like I'm brushing over it. So, let's get a vital discussion out of the way now.

As a trauma-informed coach, I've rarely met a woman who didn't have ACEs (Adverse Childhood Experiences). In my research for my psychology thesis, I found that those challenged with the phenomenon I call Driven Woman Syndrome certainly have ACEs that fostered or perhaps conditioned these Triple Trap habits. It has taken me years of work to become proficient in acknowledging my own experiences without re-visiting them. Having been there myself, I would *strongly* recommend doing any trauma or ACEs work with the help of a well-versed professional.

This may surprise you, but digging through the trunks in our proverbial closets is not always valuable. Sometimes, what we think therapy or coaching is—isn't. Simply talking about our problems can actually make them worse. Surprising, right? But when it comes to trauma specifically, there is an important step that needs to occur to make things better.

What we need to move forward from our trauma is emotional catharsis or what we might call a 'breakthrough.' This is experiencing our problems *differently* rather than simply releasing our negative energy by talking or venting about the problems. It takes a true professional to know how to guide us through our trauma to arrive at that catharsis.

Additionally, while using therapy or coaching as a way to vent through our problems may get us through the moment, it can also send our brain the 'signal' that the issue is no longer a concern and doesn't need our attention. Great, right? Nope! Our motivation for change has been all but lost. You see, our desire for dramatic change is more potent when inspired by our negative experiences. Just think back to the last time you made a significant change. Wasn't it when you finally had enough of feeling or behaving a certain way? So again, should you feel ready to get into healing around past trauma, please see a trained professional.

Okay, so that's enough on trauma for now. Of course, there is more to discuss! But as we begin our journey together, I wanted to get us on the same page about this critical subject.

The Tripple Trap

I remember the day I realized I was caught in a trap—a triple trap, to be exact. I was at the day job, sitting in yet another meeting that could have been an email, nodding along, taking meticulous notes, and mentally juggling the dozens of tasks waiting for me at home. My phone buzzed incessantly with texts: my daughter needed help sorting out her insurance at work, my client needed to move her appointment up, and a colleague in one of my classes (I was working toward my second master's degree) wanted me to cover for her on a project. Without thinking, I replied 'Yes' to all of them.

Later that night, as I was putting my dinner in the microwave at almost 10 o'clock, it hit me that I hadn't paused once to consider my own capacity or well-being. I was exhausted and stretched thin, yet I couldn't stop myself from taking on more. Why was I doing this? Why was my default response always 'Yes'?

That's when I identified the Triple Trap: Pleasing, Performing, Perfecting.

Pleasing

From a young age, many of us are conditioned to be agreeable, accommodating, and attentive to the needs of others. Saying yes becomes second nature because we fear the repercussions of disappointing someone. We worry about being seen as difficult, unhelpful, or, heaven forbid, selfish. As girls, we are often programmed to believe we are responsible for nurturing and supporting everyone around us.

I was the queen of people-pleasing. As a kid, I just wanted people to like me. My parents were young and divorced when I was just two. I was exposed to physical abuse from ages 3-5 and sexually abused before the age of twelve. I was taught that acquiescing to and pleasing a man would make my world a safer place. As an adult, the reward was my partner's happiness and, of course, that of my boss. I stayed late at work to help students and colleagues. I agreed to host family gatherings that left me drained for days afterward. My desire to make everyone happy was insatiable, and it came at the expense of my happiness.

Performing

Then there's the need to *perform*—to excel in every role we take on. We strive to be the best employee, the best mother, the best partner, and the best friend. We wear our busyness like a badge of honor, equating our worth with our productivity.

I filled every moment with activity. If I wasn't doing something 'productive,' I felt guilty. Leisure was a foreign concept. I took on extra projects at work, volunteered for committees, and enrolled in courses to further my education—all at the same time. I was in a constant state of motion, performing for an audience I wasn't even sure existed.

This need to perform is programmed early and perpetuated in the workplace. We are told that to succeed, we must take on more than our male counterparts at work and home and 'push through' any pain or challenges we might face along the way. Coming off as 'weak' or 'unable to cope' just isn't an option for most of us.

Perfecting

The final piece of the trap is *perfecting*—the relentless pursuit of flaw-lessness. Mistakes are not allowed. We hold ourselves to impossibly high standards, often higher than those we hold for others; although, they don't always see that, do they? We merely hold the bar high for those around us to get them into the same arena where we take on the lions, right?

I obsessed over details. My writing almost took on a robotic tone after editing and re-editing until the early morning hours. Nothing I worked on ever felt finished. My stress levels were through the roof. I couldn't delegate tasks because I believed no one else would do them "right." This quest for perfection was not only unrealistic but utterly exhausting.

Again, this perfectionism is baked in and then perpetuated by our cul-turescape. The quick trajectory of phones and social media hasn't helped us. It's hurting us and our children, particularly our girls. Comparisonitis is rampant, and it's a marvel that any of us feel good enough. No matter how high we climb, someone else has done it better, faster, and with more—something. And no matter what we earn, achieve, or create, we want and pursue more.

Trauma, Expectations, and Programming

Why do we fall into this triple trap? As I said, for most of us, it's rooted in past experiences and societal programming. And while my research did 'pre-qualify' many of my volunteers, I want to clarify something. Trauma doesn't always come from catastrophic events; it can stem from years of subtle messages telling us we're not enough unless we're pleasing, performing, and perfecting.

Growing up, most of us received praise when we excelled and criti-cism when we fell short. This conditioned us to seek validation through

achievement and compliance. The expectations placed upon us became the expectations we placed upon ourselves, a cycle that is hard to
break.

Our subconscious may view some of the more subtle messages as
trauma, spinning tales and making choices to do what it does best: Keep
us safe. In my first book, Ditch the Worthiness Hustle, I write more about
how I think of my subconscious as my inner supervillain. By way of quick
explanation, think of this 'critical voice' and maker of 95% of our choices
as our autopilot without adult supervision. My favorite comparison for my
subconscious is the supervillain, Harley Quinn. My goal since recognizing
and attempting to befriend my subconscious as the 'autopilot' running
established programs is: Be the adult in the room.

We Like to Do More. Don't We?

Even when we recognize we have taken on too much, we still want to
have more, do more, and be more. There's that part of us that genuinely
enjoys being capable and accomplishing tasks. We take pride in our
ability to handle multiple responsibilities. Doing more can give us a tem-
porary sense of control and fulfillment. After all, control is very important
for some of us with Driven Woman Syndrome.

But at what cost?

I began to realize that my constant need to do more was a way to distract
myself from deeper issues—feelings of inadequacy, fear of failure, and
the discomfort of stillness. By keeping busy, I didn't have to face these
uncomfortable emotions.

This behavior revealed itself in spades one evening when I watched a
man on television say something that triggered my feelings of never
being enough. I almost leaped off of my couch. I then started pacing
around my kitchen, pulling open drawers for no reason. This rather
obvious trigger reaction allowed me to catch it and become the 'adult in
the room' that night. I learned a lot from that event, but how many times

had I simply buried my emotions rather than allow myself to observe them?

It's important to remember that doing more isn't always about the thing. Sometimes, our autopilot buddy is just trying to keep us safe.

But I ask you: Is denying ourselves the right to feel things really safe?

Judgment and the Fear of Being 'Bad at Womanhood'

Underlying all of this pleasing, performing, and perfecting is the fear of judgment. We worry that if we don't uphold the age-old norms of parenting, cleanliness, and caretaking, we'll be labeled as 'bad' women. These expectations are so deeply planted in our socialscape that deviating from them feels like a personal failing.

I remember overhearing a comment when the kids were still pretty young at a school event. I had just driven through the Golden Arches drive-through, and that nugget sauce in the car was a bad call. "Did you see how disheveled her kids looked? She must have her hands full." I was mortified to realize they were talking about me. The judgment stung, reinforcing my belief that I needed to try even harder. All these years later, I still feel the twinge of not being 'good enough' at mothering.

But here's the truth: These standards are unrealistic and detrimental to our well-being. They keep us trapped in a cycle of overcommitment and self-criticism. Additionally, judging each other in this way is a trap of its own, robbing us of a much-needed sisterhood.

Breaking Free from the Triple Trap

Acknowledging the trap is the first step toward escaping it. At one point, after being conned, abused, and sapped of retirement funds *and* my mojo, I fled to Washington, and after some time with an abuse counselor and help from my Auntie, I moved to Texas with my son.

That journey with my son and his mental illness is enough to fill its own book. I will simply say that about eighteen months later, I was on my own and starting over… again.

It took a while, but when I was ready, I began questioning why I felt compelled to please everyone, perform constantly, and perfect every task. Was it making me happier? Was it improving my relationships? The answer was a resounding no. I only ended up fatigued, frustrated, and frazzled.

I finally started setting boundaries—a previously foreign word to me. I practiced saying 'No' without justification or apology. It was uncomfortable at first, but with each instance, I felt a little freer.

I set rules around relationships that were draining. Oh, I didn't share the rules with them—the rules were for me. I believe in communicating boundaries, as we will discuss. However, there are some people who only see those boundaries as a challenge. That's when it's better to focus on ourselves and what to do when *we* feel uncomfortable.

I am still constantly working on allowing myself to do things imperfectly or not at all. I must remind myself that the world will not fall apart if I give less than 100% on everything. The words, 'good enough' have crept into my vocabulary.

Recently, I listened to a podcast where the coach stated that we are only at our peak for 2-3 hours a day. He asked, "Why give those hours to someone else when you should reserve them for your passion project?"

This is an incredibly fair question. After all, isn't our 60-80% really more by other people's standards anyway? Couldn't we devote our best two to three hours to the life-changing thing that evokes passion and excitement for us?

Stealing little moments for myself is another new habit of mine. Creating a habit of staying connected to myself has been the most important thing I've done in my life. These precious mini-breaks are spent creating joy without a productive purpose—reading for 20-30 minutes, taking a leisurely walk, or simply sitting quietly on the balcony with a cup of tea in the morning.

Self-Reflection Exercise: Recognizing Your Triple Trap

Okay, Soul Sister. I invite you to reflect on your own life. Are you caught in the triple trap of pleasing, performing, and perfecting? Grab your journal and consider the following questions:

- *Pleasing:* Do you often say 'Yes' when you want to say 'No'? Are you afraid of disappointing others? Who?

- *Performing:* Do you equate your worth with how much you accomplish? Do you feel guilty when you're not being 'productive'? Do you feel you have to be everything to everyone in *both* the professional and personal realms of your life?

- *Perfecting:* Do you hold yourself to impossibly high standards? Are you overly critical of your mistakes? Where in your life do you see this pattern? Do you find that you hold others to a higher standard as well? Do the people around you find it difficult to keep up?

Write down your thoughts. Recognizing these patterns is the first step toward changing them.

Moving Forward

Breaking free from the triple trap isn't easy. It requires patience, self-compassion, and a willingness to challenge deeply ingrained beliefs. But the freedom that comes with it is immeasurable. I'd love to tell you that this is a one-time breakthrough. It's not. This programming runs deep, and your subconscious has put in a lot of work creating behavior responses that it believes keep you safe. This will take constant care, like a beautiful garden or Bonsai tree in your kitchen window.

As we continue this journey together, remember that you are not alone. We all struggle with these traps in one way or another. But by acknowledging them, we take back control of our lives and move closer to the peace and fulfillment we truly desire.

In the next chapter, we'll explore how overcommitment manifests in our lives and the energetic toll it takes. We'll delve into who gets your best and who gets what's left, helping you choose the 'irons in your fire' more intentionally.

Let's continue this journey toward embracing our limitations and finding true greatness in the freedom of not having it all.

Chapter 2

The Energetics of Overcommitment

I used to believe that time was my most precious resource. I meticulously scheduled every hour, juggling work commitments, family obligations, social events, and personal projects. My calendar was a colorful tapestry of appointments and to-do lists, each a testament to my ability to 'do it all' and be 'everything to everyone.' However, I always felt drained, no matter how efficiently I managed my time. It wasn't until I started paying attention to my energy—not just my time—that I realized the true cost of overcommitment.

Energy Matters: Who Gets Your Best and Who Gets What's Left?

Have you ever noticed how some activities leave you feeling invigorated while others leave you exhausted? It's not just about the physical effort involved; it's about the energetic exchange. Every interaction, task, and thought consumes energy. When we're overcommitted, we often give our best energy to tasks and people that may not align with our true priorities, leaving little for what truly matters to us.

For years, I gave my prime hours to my job, believing that was the path to success and stability. I poured myself into projects, stayed late to meet deadlines, and took on extra work to prove my worth. By the time I got home, I was depleted. My family got the leftovers—the tired smiles, the half-hearted conversations, the constant promises of 'Maybe later' because I inevitably brought work home with me.

It wasn't just work that sapped my energy. I found myself saying 'Yes' to social engagements I didn't enjoy, volunteering for committees out of a sense of obligation, and even engaging in hobbies that no longer brought me joy simply because I didn't want to disappoint others or let go of past identities.

The truth is energy is a finite resource. Unlike time, which marches on regardless of how we feel, our energy levels fluctuate and can be renewed or depleted based on how we *choose* to spend them. Recognizing this was a game-changer for me.

The Invisible Drain

Overcommitment doesn't just happen in our schedules; it happens in our minds and hearts. We carry mental to-do lists, worry about others' opinions, and replay past conversations, all of which consume energy. Emotional labor—the unseen effort of managing not just our own feelings but often those of others—is a significant yet frequently unacknowledged drain.

I recall a period when a close friend was going through a tough time. I wanted to be there for her, and I was—day or night, I made myself available. But I neglected to acknowledge how supporting her was affecting my emotional well-being. I didn't set boundaries, and eventually, I found myself feeling resentful and fatigued. It wasn't her fault; I hadn't communicated my limits or taken responsibility for managing my own energy.

Choosing Your Irons in the Fire

We've all heard the saying, "Too many irons in the fire." For the longest time, I took pride in having as many irons as possible. It made me feel important, needed, and in control. But in reality, I was spreading myself so thin that none of my irons were heating properly. I was busy but not necessarily effective or fulfilled.

One day, I sat down and listed all the commitments and responsibilities I had taken on. The list was overwhelming. I realized that many of these 'irons' were things I didn't even care about deeply; I had taken them on out of obligation, habit, or fear of missing out.

I asked myself a pivotal question: "Who gets my best, and who gets what's left?"

This self-reflection led me to make some tough decisions. I stepped down from a committee that no longer resonated with me. I declined new projects at work that didn't align with my interests or career goals. I even had to stop working on a hobby. I realized it had become another obligation I was only pursuing because I'd already invested so much time.

By choosing intentionally where to focus my energy, I found that I was not only more effective but also more content. I had more energy to give to the people and activities that genuinely mattered to me.

The Ripple Effect of Overcommitment

Overcommitment doesn't just affect us; it impacts those around us. When constantly drained, we're not showing up as our best selves for our loved ones, colleagues, or ourselves.

Our patience wears thin, our creativity diminishes, and our capacity for joy shrinks.

I remember snapping at my daughter over something trivial—a misplaced shoe or a spilled drink. The look on her face was one of surprise and hurt. At that moment, I realized that my exhaustion was spilling over into my relationships, causing unintended harm. I wish I could say that was the only time that occurred. It wasn't. Looking back, I still wish I could retract those moments.

By constantly operating in a state of overcommitment, we also model this behavior for those around us, perpetuating a cycle where busyness is equated with worthiness. Do we want our children or peers to believe that they must run themselves ragged to be valued? Upon reflection, I remember many occasions when a friend or group of friends and I were gabbing about how busy we were. It was almost as if we were displaying our wartime medals to each other. Oh, you too?

Energy Vampires

You know these people. I bet you are seeing someone in your mind right now. So why do we allow them to enter our space and drain our energy? You know why. Just like I know why. Sometimes, it's because they are our boss or family member. We don't want to pay the consequences of removing them from our lives or erecting some boundaries. But what about the others?

Perhaps we don't want to appear mean or unjust. Or, like myself and so many of my clients, you just aren't comfortable with confrontation. It's icky and awkward, right? Sure, we may feel completely fine engaging with a subordinate about work matters, but telling a friend her behaviors are toxic? That's a different story for so many of us. Here's what I want to continue saying as we move forward: Boundaries with some people are better left unsaid. This group of people most certainly qualify. We'll get into boundaries more deeply later, but do write their names down in these exercises and begin to consider how you can quietly erect boundaries that serve you.

Reclaiming Your Energy

So, how do we begin to reclaim our energy? It starts with awareness and a willingness to make changes.

Self-Reflection Exercise: Love It or Leave It (aka Hell yes or hell no)

I invite you to take some time to reflect on your commitments. Grab a journal or a piece of paper and make two columns:

- Love It (hell, yes): List the activities, responsibilities, and relationships that energize you, bring you joy, and align with your values.

- Leave It (hell, no): List those that drain you, feel obligatory, or no longer serve your growth. Don't forget the vampires!

Be honest with yourself. This exercise isn't about immediate action but about gaining clarity.

Once you've completed your lists, consider:

- What can you delegate or eliminate from your 'Leave It' list?

- How can you create more space for the things on your 'Love It' list?

- Are there boundaries you need to set to protect your energy?

Remember, saying 'No' to one thing is saying 'Yes' to something else—often your own well-being. And just in case you are muttering that not everything we do is supposed to bring us joy, know that as a Gen-Xer, I value hard work and understand that programming well.

But listen, if it doesn't bring you joy—or make you holler, "Hell yes!" doesn't that activity, person, or project at least deserve a temp spot in the 'leave it' column? You can always bring it/them back if you find it necessary. Okay. That's the end of the lecture.

The Power of Prioritization

Understanding where our energy goes allows us to prioritize more effectively. It's not just about doing less but doing more of what matters.

This may require tough choices and uncomfortable conversations, but the payoff is immense.

When I began prioritizing my energy, I noticed significant improvements in my life. I had more patience with my loved ones, more creativity in my work, and more joy in my daily experiences. I was no longer merely surviving my days but actively engaging with them.

Push Back

Yep. It's going to happen. There will be people in your life who just aren't comfortable with changes in your attitudes, boundaries, or decisions to prioritize you and your energy. Guess what? That's going to have to be okay. This work, all the work, is about you and your happiness, energy, and fulfillment, right? Making sure *everyone* is happy with *everything* is no longer your job. We left that job description in the wastebasket the moment you picked up this book.

So here's what you say to anyone who expresses frustration about your renewed commitment to yourself: Thanks for the feedback. I'll take it under advisement.

Embracing the Flow

Energy management isn't about rigid schedules or strict limitations; it's about tuning into and honoring your natural rhythms, sometimes literally. During each 28-day cycle (yes, even after menopause), you may have days with abundant energy to tackle multiple tasks; other days, rest may be the most productive thing you can do.

Here's a little exercise you can do: For the next ten days, notice how often you tell yourself to do things like 'push through' or, my personal favorite, 'just keep swimming.' These are learned behaviors and not always what is best for us. Seriously.

By embracing this natural ebb and flow, we can move away from the constant push of overcommitment and toward a more sustainable and fulfilling way of living. Taking time to recharge or allowing decompression time will likely make us even *more* productive and successful.

Closing Thoughts

Our culture often celebrates overcommitment as a sign of ambition and dedication, but it can come at the expense of our health, happiness, and relationships. By paying attention to the energetics of overcommitment, we can make conscious choices that honor our true selves.

Remember, your energy is precious. You have the right and the power to decide where it goes. When you choose to invest it in alignment with your values and desires, you enrich your own life and positively impact those around you.

Let's continue this journey together, exploring how to reclaim our energy, set meaningful priorities, and embrace the freedom of not having it all.

In the next chapter, we'll delve into the invisible weight of expectations— the unspoken pressures from society, family, and ourselves that often drive us to overcommit. We'll explore how to recognize these expectations and begin the process of leaning away from programming that doesn't serve us.

Chapter 3

The Invisible Weight of Expectations

I remember feeling like I was carrying the weight of the world. It wasn't just the responsibilities of work, family, or personal commitments—it was something less tangible but far heavier: the unspoken expectations of others and the relentless demands I placed on myself.

The Unspoken Expectations of Others and Self

From an early age, we're surrounded by expectations. Family, friends, society—all have their ideas of who we should be and how we should live our lives. As women, these expectations can be particularly suffocating. We're expected to be nurturing yet strong, ambitious yet selfless, independent yet accommodating. It's a delicate balancing act, and the tightrope we're walking is often strung with invisible threads of expectation.

For me, these expectations manifested in countless ways. I felt the need to excel professionally while also being the perfect mother, friend, and partner. I believed I had to maintain a pristine home, cook gourmet meals, have baked cookies ready for the kids when they got home, and, of course, look put-together at all times. It almost sounds ridiculous reading it, doesn't it? But the pressure was immense, and much of it was self-imposed.

But where did these expectations come from? Some were inherited from family values, while others were absorbed by societal norms portrayed in media and our culturescape. Over time, they became so ingrained that I couldn't distinguish between what I truly wanted and felt I *should* want.

A Client's Journey: Grayson's Story

Let me share the story of Grayson, a client whose experience mirrors what so many of us go through. Grayson was a high-achieving professional in her mid-thirties, working as a marketing executive at a prestigious firm. She was also a mother of two young children pursuing a part-time MBA. From the outside, Grayson appeared to have it all together—a thriving career, a beautiful family, and ambitious goals.

But when Grayson came to me, she was on the edge of burnout. She confessed that she felt like she was constantly failing. At work, she pushed herself to outperform, often staying late to perfect presentations. At home, she tried to be the ideal mother, baking cupcakes for school events, organizing playdates, and ensuring her home was Instagram-worthy. She also felt compelled to maintain an active social life, attend networking events, and keep up with friends.

"I feel like I'm drowning," she told me during one of our sessions. "No matter how much I do, it's never enough. I'm exhausted, but I can't seem to slow down. Everyone expects so much from me, and I don't want to let them down."

As we delved deeper, it became clear that Grayson was grappling with the invisible weight of expectations—from her parents, who had always emphasized the importance of hard work and success; from her colleagues, who admired her dedication and reliability; from her friends, who saw her as the glue that held their group together; and most significantly, from herself.

Grayson had internalized these expectations to the point where she believed that her worth was directly tied to her ability to meet them. The thought of disappointing anyone was unbearable to her.

Leaning Away from the Programming

Breaking free from these expectations requires us to first recognize them. It's like peeling back layers of an onion—each layer reveals another belief or assumption we've internalized without question.

With Grayson, we began by identifying the sources of her expectations. I asked her to make a list of all the 'shoulds' in her life. Her list included statements like:

> "I should always be available for my children."

> "I should be the top performer at work."

> "I should keep my home immaculate."

> "I should continue advancing my education."

> "I should never let others see me struggle."

Seeing these expectations written down was a revelation for Grayson. She realized that many of these 'shoulds' weren't rooted in her own desires but were absorbed from external sources—her parents' emphasis on achievement, societal ideals of motherhood, her partner's expectations, and the relentless portrayal of 'having it all' in media.

There was one more 'should' on Grayson's list:

> "I should be happy."

As she wrote that sentence, Grayson started to cry. She apologized, and I suggested she just allow herself to feel whatever was going on there. I told her to grab the tissues and settle in. A few minutes later, Grayson and I chatted about what she had been feeling.

"It's so crazy that this list made me realize it," Grayson said. "But I'm not happy living like this. No matter where I go, I feel like I'm letting someone down. And when I wrote that I *should* be happy? It suddenly hit me that I have been letting myself down the most. All those promises I made to *me*—I don't think I've kept a single one."

That was the day that Grayson had her catharsis.

Grayson continued the exercise by questioning each expectation:

- Why do I believe this?

- Is this expectation serving me or harming me?

- What would happen if I let go of this expectation?

As she reflected, Grayson began to see how these ingrained beliefs were incredibly unrealistic and also detrimental to her well-being. She was also able to recognize that her childhood experiences provided some of the foundation for these beliefs. In some cases, merely to provide a *different* experience for her own children.

Do You Communicate Your Boundaries?

One of the most significant steps in shedding the weight of expectations is learning to set and communicate boundaries. For a long time, Grayson struggled with this, just as I had done. There's a genuine fear that saying 'no' or expressing our true feelings will lead to conflict or rejection.

Grayson realized she rarely communicated her needs or limits to others. At work, she took on extra projects without protest, fearing that declining would make her seem less committed. Worse, like so many of us, she had been programmed to believe that success *relied* on saying yes to virtually all requests for fear of being passed over for promotion. At home, she managed the majority of household responsibilities because she wanted to be the one who had it all together. Later, she realized it was also because she didn't really *trust* her partner with these tasks.

We discussed the importance of setting boundaries—not as a way to push others away but as a means to protect her energy and prioritize her well-being.

Grayson decided to start small. She spoke with her partner about sharing household tasks more equitably. To her surprise, he was more than willing to help but hadn't realized she felt overwhelmed because she hadn't expressed it. Next, she approached her supervisor at work, explaining that while she was committed to her role, she needed to manage her workload to maintain high-quality output.

Communicating boundaries doesn't have to be confrontational. It's about expressing your needs clearly and respectfully. It's a form of self-respect and, ultimately, fosters healthier relationships.

A terrific mantra I often repeat is, "Boundaries with grace."

Self-Reflection Exercise: What Are Your Boundaries?

I invite you to reflect on your own boundaries. Consider the following questions:

- Where in your life do you feel overextended or taken advantage of?

- Are there situations where you consistently ignore your needs to meet others' expectations?

- What are your non-negotiables—things that you need to protect your well-being?

- Are there 'quiet' boundaries to consider for those individuals who you know would only see your boundary statements as a challenge?

- What are the potential consequences of erecting these boundaries? Are they worth it? If so, how will you prepare yourself for a) dealing with those consequences or b) the inevitable pushback?

There are different ways to organize boundaries. One way you might consider is to draw a series of circles and attach 'rules' and then people to each. The innermost circle is your 'safe space' or sanctuary. The space for your private thoughts and dreams. Perhaps the next circle contains your partner or children, then your parents. For each section, decide what resources are available to each group or person and which are restricted or excluded.

I always reserve an 'outer space' area for those who aren't entirely removed from my life but are given severely restricted access.

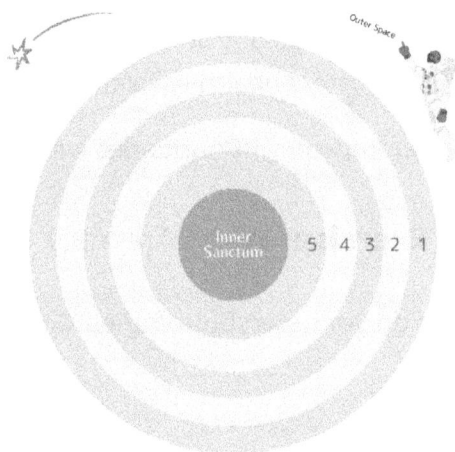

Example on classification of 'zones': You may decide Saturday morning is only for you and your partner, and phones are off. You may decide Sunday mornings are for the kids or best friend or time with a good book and a cuppa.

You may also decide that each zone represents levels of access or trust. It's entirely up to you.

Another way to reflect on boundaries may be to draw some columns and list the boundaries you deem most essential and the associated people underneath.

One client of mine decided through this exercise that starting on sundown Friday; it was a digital Sabbath. If someone wanted to get ahold of her, they'd have to wait until Saturday nightfall. While not Jewish, the idea of a day of rest at the end of the work week really appealed to her. Sure, she found it difficult at first. After a while, though, she realized that without the phone in hand, she just felt healthier and more intentional about her own peace of mind.

The Fear of Disappointing Others

The fear of disappointing others is a significant barrier to setting boundaries and releasing expectations. We worry about being perceived as selfish, unkind, or uncooperative. This fear can be deeply rooted in our desire for acceptance and belonging.

Grayson struggled with this fear. She worried that by setting boundaries, she would let people down or damage her relationships. However, as she began communicating her needs, she found that most people were understanding and supportive.

Of course, not everyone reacted positively. A colleague who was used to Grayson picking up the slack was annoyed when she declined additional work. A friend seemed put off when Grayson couldn't attend a social gathering that fell on a 'family' day. But Grayson learned she couldn't control others' reactions—she could only be true to herself.

Here's the truth: You cannot pour from an empty cup. Continuously prioritizing others' expectations at the expense of your own needs is unsustainable and ultimately detrimental to all involved.

Letting Go of Self-Imposed Expectations

While external expectations are significant, the expectations we place on ourselves can be even more burdensome. We often hold ourselves to impossibly high standards, striving for perfection in every area of life.

Grayson realized that her harshest critic was herself. She felt that she was failing unless she excelled in all areas. This black-and-white thinking left little room for self-compassion.

I encouraged Grayson to practice self-kindness. We worked on reframing her thoughts:

- Instead of "I didn't finish that project on time; I'm incompetent," she practiced saying, "I faced unexpected challenges, but I did my best under the circumstances."

- Instead of "I missed my son's soccer game; I'm a terrible mother," she reminded herself, "I attend as many games as I can, and my son knows I support him."

Practicing self-compassion doesn't mean making excuses; it means acknowledging our humanity. We all have limitations, and that's okay.

Embracing Your Authentic Self

As Grayson shed the layers of external and internal expectations, she began reconnecting with her authentic self. She rediscovered passions that had been sidelined, like painting and hiking. She started to make choices based on her values rather than others' approval.

One significant change Grayson made was adjusting her pursuit of an MBA. She realized she was doing it more out of a sense of obligation than genuine desire. After much consideration, she decided to pause her studies. This decision freed up time and mental space, allowing her to focus on what truly mattered to her.

Grayson's relationships improved as well. By being open about her needs and boundaries, she fostered deeper connections based on mutual respect and understanding.

The Impact on Mental and Emotional Health

The invisible weight of expectations doesn't just affect our schedules—it takes a toll on our mental and emotional health. Chronic stress from trying to meet unrealistic expectations can lead to anxiety, depression, and severe physical health issues.

In Grayson's case, she had been experiencing insomnia, headaches, and a persistent feeling of anxiety. As she began to release these expectations and prioritize self-care, her symptoms gradually improved. She reported feeling lighter, more present, and more joyful.

Breaking the Cycle for Future Generations

One powerful motivation for all of us can be the desire to model healthier behaviors for our children, friends, or family. You know the old saying? Lead by example.

By embracing authenticity and setting boundaries, perhaps we can empower those around us to value themselves beyond external achievements and societal pressures. Maybe we can even inspire someone to put down their phone for a few precious hours.

Closing Thoughts

The invisible weight of expectations can be a heavy burden, but it doesn't have to define our lives. By becoming aware of these expectations, setting boundaries, and practicing self-compassion, we can release this weight and step into a life that reflects our true selves.

Remember, it's not about shirking responsibilities or disregarding others' feelings. It's about finding a balance that honors both your needs and your relationships.

Self-Reflection Exercise: Leaning Away from the Programming

- Identify one expectation—either from others or yourself—that feels burdensome.

- Ask yourself: Where does this expectation come from? Is it aligned with my current values and desires?

- Consider one small step you can take to challenge or release this expectation.

Moving Forward

Breaking free from the invisible weight of expectations is an ongoing journey. There will be times when old patterns resurface, or you face resistance from others. That's okay. Change takes time, and every step you take toward authenticity is progress.

As we continue this journey together, remember that you are not alone. Many of us grapple with these challenges, and by sharing our stories and supporting one another, we can create a community that values genuine connections over superficial expectations.

Letting go of these weights doesn't mean you care less—it means you care deeply about living a life that's true to who you are.

In the next chapter, we'll explore the cost of striving for an unattainable ideal. We'll examine how pursuing 'having it all' impacts our health, relationships, and overall well-being. Together, we'll uncover strategies to redefine success on your own terms and cultivate a more balanced, fulfilling life.

Chapter 4

The Cost of Having It All

I used to wear my overcommitment like a badge of honor. Juggling a demanding career, family responsibilities, social obligations, and personal projects, I believed that keeping all the balls in the air was a testament to my strength and capability. But beneath the façade of 'having it all,' I was slowly unraveling. The relentless pursuit of an unattainable ideal took a toll on every aspect of my life.

At What Cost?

The idea of 'having it all' is seductive. Society tells us that we can and should strive to excel in every domain of our lives. It's almost become some kind of contest on social media. The gal with the most balls in the air wins. But this pursuit often comes at a significant cost—physically, mentally, and emotionally. Let's explore the tangible impacts of this relentless striving, not just through personal anecdotes but also by examining the broader picture.

The Free-Time Gender Gap

According to the Free-Time Gender Gap Report by the Global Economic Policy Institute (GEPI), women worldwide spend significantly more time on unpaid domestic work than men. This includes cooking, cleaning, childcare, and eldercare. The report highlights that, on average, women have 4.5 hours less free time per week compared to men. This disparity persists across different countries and cultures, a stark reminder of the invisible labor that women often shoulder.[1]

This constant juggling of professional and domestic responsibilities leaves little room for rest or self-care. The expectation to manage both spheres flawlessly is not just unrealistic but also harmful. It perpetuates a cycle where women's time is undervalued, and their contributions are taken for granted.

Mental Health and Burnout

A recent survey by Deloitte revealed that 48% of women are concerned or very concerned about their mental health. Women are more likely to experience burnout than men and report that they are not receiving adequate mental health support in the workplace. The pressure to perform at high levels in all areas of life contributes to chronic stress, anxiety, and depression.[2]

In my own life, the work I've done in this area hasn't inoculated me from the overwhelm caused by the sheer volume of tasks in a typical day as a professional with two businesses to run. It is still something I must constantly manage. Being strict about a sleep schedule connects to my ability to start the day early, which connects to my ability to workout, meditate, and journal in the mornings, which connects to my overall happiness. Throughout the years, I've discovered that my morning and evening routines make or break the rest of my day.

The National Alliance on Mental Illness (NAMI) reports that burnout is particularly prevalent among women aged 50-64, but it affects women

---

[1] Gpmain@thegepi.org, "The Free-Time Gender Gap," Gender Equity Policy Institute (GEPI), October 3, 2024, https://thegepi.org/the-free-time-gender-gap/

[2] "Deloitte Women @ Work 2024: A Global Outlook," Deloitte, 2024, https://www.deloitte.com/global/en/issues/work/content/women-at-work-global-outlook.html

across all age groups. Barriers to seeking professional help include financial constraints, fear of social judgment, and a lack of awareness.[3]

Health Challenges

Beyond mental health, there are significant physical health implications. Approximately 27% of women have experienced challenges related to menstruation, menopause, or fertility, according to Deloitte's research. Many women work through pain without taking time off, often because they feel they cannot afford to show any signs of weakness or vulnerability in the workplace and many who simply can't afford to take time off.

I remember pushing through severe migraines and chronic back pain, fueled by the belief that taking a day off would be seen as unprofessional or would put my job at risk. This 'push through' mentality is pervasive and damaging. My female supervisor did nothing to mitigate this fear, even when my symptoms led to a more serious illness.

My situation was not uncommon. Women are less likely to feel comfortable discussing physical and mental health challenges with managers, leading to isolation and worsening of symptoms. The stigma surrounding women's health issues perpetuates silence and neglect, preventing necessary accommodations and support.

Domestic Responsibilities and the Double Shift

Women continue to take on a disproportionate share of domestic responsibilities, even when they are employed full-time. This 'double shift' means that after a full day of work, many women return home to a second round of tasks—cooking, cleaning, and caring for children or elderly relatives.

3   "The 2024 Nami Workplace Mental Health Poll," NAMI, May 9, 2024, https://www.nami.org/support-education/publications-reports/survey-reports/the-2024-nami-workplace-mental-health-poll/#:~:text=Burnout%20is%20a%20problem%2C%20especially, 50%2D64%20said%20the%20same

This imbalance negatively impacts careers and mental health. The time and energy spent on unpaid domestic work limit opportunities for rest, professional development, and leisure activities that are crucial for our well-being.

You know how it is—a full day of work, dinner, groceries, housework, and more. If you have kids, it's also pick-ups, drop-offs, homework, and appointments. If you're anything like me, you've tried all the calendars and planners, trying to 'time-manage' your way through it. We buy into the notion that *we* must be the problem. We believe if we can only become super-arrangers of the mere 24 hours allotted, we can keep our balls in the air.

The Personal and Professional Toll

The cumulative effect of these factors is profound. Striving for an unattainable ideal of being it all, doing it all, and having it all leads to:

- Chronic Stress and Burnout: Prolonged stress without adequate recovery time leads to burnout, affecting physical and mental health.

- Relationship Strain: Overcommitment can strain relationships with family, friends, and colleagues due to lack of time, energy, and presence.

- Decreased Productivity and Job Satisfaction: Ironically, the effort to excel in the workplace can lead to reduced productivity due to exhaustion and diminished cognitive function.

- Loss of Self: Constantly meeting others' expectations can disconnect us from our authentic selves, passions, and desires.

A Deeper Look: Rena's Story

Let me introduce you to Rena, another client whose experience illuminates the hidden costs of having it all. Rena was a married senior manager at a tech company, with one child in elementary school. She prided herself on being efficient and organized, often multitasking to maximize productivity.

However, Rena began experiencing panic attacks. They would strike unexpectedly—in meetings, while driving, and even during family dinners. She couldn't understand why this was happening. She was doing everything 'right,' following the blueprint for success.

In our sessions, Rena uncovered that her relentless schedule left no room for processing emotions or stress. She moved from one task to the next without pause, and when exhaustion or subtle stress symptoms occurred, she forced herself to 'push through it.' These panic attacks were her body's way of signaling that something was profoundly wrong.

Rena also realized that she rarely spent quality time with her daughter. Despite being physically present, work and upcoming obligations always occupied her mind. Often bringing work home, she would make empty promises and then beat herself up for not delivering.

We worked on strategies to create space in her life—both mentally and physically. Rena began setting firm boundaries around her work hours, delegating tasks (one of the most challenging things for driven women), and prioritizing downtime. She practiced mindfulness routines to reconnect with herself, and started actively working to be more present with her family.

Over time, Rena's panic attacks subsided. She reported feeling more grounded and connected. She gained a more profound sense of fulfillment by relinquishing the need to do everything perfectly.

The Cultural Narrative

The pressure to have it all is deeply embedded in our cultural narrative. Media, advertising, and even well-intentioned role models often portray an idealized version of womanhood where career success, family happiness, social engagement, and personal wellness are all seamlessly integrated.

This narrative fails to acknowledge the structural inequalities and unrealistic expectations placed on women. It ignores the support systems that make such balancing acts possible for some—such as wealth, staff, or flexible schedules—not accessible to all.

By perpetuating this myth, we inadvertently promote a standard that is unattainable for most and harmful when pursued without consideration of personal limits and well-being.

Redefining Success

The notion of having it all is based on external definitions of success—prestigious careers, perfect families, and social status. As technology advances, our socialcape has become increasingly focused on external ideals of happiness. But what if we shifted the focus to what truly brings us fulfillment and joy?

Success doesn't have to mean doing everything perfectly or meeting all societal expectations. It can be about living authentically, nurturing meaningful relationships, and taking care of our well-being.

For me, redefining success meant letting go of the need to prove myself through constant achievement. It meant taking a year away from one of my businesses to prioritize my health and reevaluate how I would move forward. Initially, I felt like a failure and needed a break. As the months passed, I had some dark moments, even questioning if I should close the business for good.

It took almost a year, but I refocused on valuing quality over quantity, presence over productivity, and self-compassion over self-criticism.

Cultivating Self-Compassion

Self-compassion is one of the most potent tools in countering the cost of having it all. At a recent talk on the topic, almost the entire audience nodded when I said that we all need to practice it more, so why aren't we all including it as part of our experience? Sadly, practicing self-compassion isn't always easy because it involves treating ourselves with the same kindness and understanding we would offer a friend.

When working with clients, part of our work together involves imagining our critical voice and subconscious, not only as our inner supervillain but also as our friend who needs a great deal of support and compassion. When we talk about 'being the adult in the room,' it is about grace, love, and forgiveness as much as leadership, strength, and accountability.

Self-compassion allows us to acknowledge our struggles without judgment. It creates space for rest and healing. It reminds us that imperfection is part of the human experience.

Practicing self-compassion can take many forms:

- Mindful Awareness: Paying attention to our feelings and needs without judgment.

- Allowing: Letting our feelings exist without analyzing or going deep.

- Self-Kindness: Offering ourselves words of encouragement and understanding.

- Sisterhood: Recognizing that we are not alone in our struggles.

Building a Support Network

Creating a supportive community around ourselves is essential. Whether it's friends, family, colleagues, or professional networks, having people who understand and validate our experiences makes a significant difference.

Support networks provide:

- Emotional Support: A safe space to express feelings and fears.

- Practical Assistance: Help with tasks or responsibilities.

- Accountability: Encouragement to set boundaries and prioritize well-being.

Embracing "Good Enough"

Letting go of perfectionism is liberating. Embracing the concept of "good enough" allows us to focus on what truly matters and accept that we cannot excel in all areas simultaneously.

This doesn't mean settling for mediocrity but recognizing our limitations and prioritizing our energy.

Self-Reflection Exercise: The Wheel of Life

The Wheel of Life is a tool used to assess balance across different areas of life. It can help identify where you're thriving and where you may need attention.

Draw a Circle: Divide it into eight sections, like a pie.

Label Each Section: Common categories include:

- Career

- Family

- Relationships

- Health

- Personal Growth

- Recreation/Fun

- Finances

- Physical Environment (home, workspaces)

Rate Each Area: On a scale from 1 to 10, rate your satisfaction in each area.

Reflect:

- Which areas are flourishing?

- Which areas are lacking?

- How does striving for 'having it all' impact these areas?

Set Intentions:

- Choose one or two areas to focus on improving.

- Identify small, actionable steps to enhance satisfaction in those areas.

Creating Your Own Definition of 'All'

Perhaps it's time to redefine what 'having it all' means to you personally. This may involve:

- Aligning with Values: Identify your core values and ensure your actions reflect them.

- Setting Realistic Goals: Establish achievable objectives that honor your well-being.

- Prioritize Joy and Fulfillment: Engage in activities and relationships that bring genuine happiness.

Closing Thoughts

The journey toward redefining success and reclaiming our lives is not easy. It requires courage, self-reflection, and sometimes difficult conversations. But the alternative—continuing to sacrifice our well-being for an illusion—is far more costly.

Remember, you are not alone in this journey. Many of us are grappling with these challenges, and together, we can support one another in creating a more balanced, fulfilling life.

It's okay to let some balls drop. It's okay to rest. It's okay to say no. By embracing these truths, we open ourselves up to a life that's not just survivable but truly livable.

In the next chapter, we'll delve into recognizing unacknowledged trauma and how it influences our choices. We'll explore how allowing those parts of ourselves out of the closet—but not into the arena—can lead to healing and a deeper understanding of ourselves.

Chapter 5

Recognizing Unacknowledged Trauma

Reflecting on specific moments, I realize that not all wounds announce themselves with grand gestures or dramatic flair. Some of the most profound impacts come from the subtle, almost imperceptible experiences that quietly shape our inner world. These unacknowledged traumas—the silent undercurrents—often influence our behaviors, choices, and relationships in ways we might not fully understand.

I remember when a simple offhand comment from a colleague sent me spiraling into self-doubt. It was a busy Tuesday afternoon, and we were reviewing a project I'd worked tirelessly on.

"This is okay, but maybe consider adding more information from the work I did to support your conclusions," she said casually.

On the surface, it was constructive feedback, but internally, I felt a wave of inadequacy wash over me. I spent the rest of the day questioning my abilities, replaying the conversation, and wondering why such a small remark had such a big impact.

It wasn't until I took a step back and reflected that I began to understand what was happening. That comment had touched a nerve linked to past experiences—times when I felt 'not good enough' or my efforts were dismissed. These feelings weren't just about the present moment; they were echoes from earlier chapters of my life.

Understanding the Invisible Scars

Trauma isn't always the result of catastrophic events. Often, it's the accumulation of smaller hurts—the overlooked achievements, the unmet emotional needs, the instances when our voices weren't heard. These experiences can leave invisible scars that influence how we see ourselves and interact with the world.

Consider the metaphor of a tree. A tree can bear the marks of storms, droughts, and seasons of abundance. While it continues to grow, the rings within tell a story of its experiences. Similarly, we carry within us the stories of our past—the joys, the pains, the lessons—all contributing to who we are today.

In my professional journey, I've met many women who, like me, carried unacknowledged traumas. One client, Annette, came to me feeling constantly overwhelmed and anxious. She was successful in her career, had a loving family, and was thriving by all outward appearances. Yet, she struggled with a pervasive sense of unease.

As we delved deeper, Annette shared that she often felt like an imposter at work, fearing that others would discover she wasn't as competent as they believed. This imposter syndrome traced back to her childhood when praise was scarce, and criticism was abundant. Recognizing this connection was a pivotal moment for her. It allowed her to see that her current feelings were not a reflection of her true capabilities but were rooted in past experiences.

The Subconscious Mind's Role

Our subconscious mind is mighty. It stores all our memories, emotions, and beliefs, even those we're unaware of. These subconscious influences can drive our reactions and decisions without us realizing it.

For example, if you were taught early on that expressing emotions was a sign of weakness, you might suppress your feelings as an adult. This suppression can lead to stress, anxiety, and a disconnect from your authentic self.

By bringing these subconscious patterns into our conscious awareness, we gain the opportunity to address and heal them.

Allowing Yourself to Feel

One of the challenges with unacknowledged trauma is that we often avoid confronting it. We might tell ourselves to 'keep it together' or 'stay strong,' pushing aside uncomfortable emotions. However, healing requires us to acknowledge and process these feelings.

Not long enough ago, I was constantly swimming in 'busy,' filling every moment with work, social events, or distractions. Even my favorite hobby was filled with to-do lists. I hadn't noticed that I had fallen back into the old habits until my daughter and I talked about how tired I was. She said in passing that even my hobby seemed like another job.

I realized I hadn't practiced daily meditation for far too long, and I knew from experience that I was running from something. Taking the time to pause and reflect, I began to uncover feelings of grief and loss that I'd been avoiding.

My son has been gone for six years. I mentioned this in chapter one. But not knowing anything had allowed me to deny any grief at all. I hadn't even permitted myself to experience the grief of his absence from my life. I'm still on the journey, but when the feelings of grief start to come, I no longer try to hold them at bay. Allowing myself to experience these emotions is challenging but ultimately freeing.

Let me ask you, when was the last time you sat with your feelings?

Strategies for Healing

Healing from unacknowledged trauma is a personal journey, and there's no one-size-fits-all approach. However, there are some strategies that can support you along the way:

- Mindfulness and Meditation: Practicing mindfulness helps you stay present and observe your thoughts and feelings without judgment. Even a few minutes a day can make a difference.

- Journaling: Writing down your thoughts provides an outlet for processing emotions. It can reveal patterns and insights that might not surface otherwise.

- Therapeutic Support: Working with a trained therapist or coach offers a safe space to explore deeper issues with professional guidance.

- Creative Expression: Engaging in art, music, dance, or writing allows you to express emotions nonverbally, tapping into different aspects of your psyche.

- Physical Activity: Exercise releases endorphins and can help reduce stress. Activities like yoga, walking, or swimming combine physical movement with mental relaxation.

- Recent studies show that tapping is a terrific way to release feelings in the body.

- Connecting with Others: Sharing your experiences with trusted friends or support groups can alleviate feelings of isolation and provide mutual encouragement.

Catching the Critical Voice

When negative thoughts arise, try to counter them with gentle affirmations. For instance, if you catch yourself thinking, "I'm not good enough," you might respond internally with, "I'm doing my best, and that's enough." This practice can gradually shift your inner dialogue toward a more positive and supportive tone.

Embracing Your Authentic Self

As you begin to acknowledge and heal unrecognized traumas, you may reconnect with parts of yourself that were previously suppressed or ignored.

Here are a few tips:

- Identify Your Values: What matters most to you? Aligning your actions with your values fosters integrity and satisfaction.

- Pursue Your Interests: Engage in activities that excite and inspire you without worrying about external approval.

- Express Yourself Honestly: Share your thoughts and feelings openly with those you trust.

Sometimes, reengaging with a hobby or artistic passion can help us reconnect with ourselves. Picking up that crochet you tried once or even something simple like coloring can be a terrific way to engage with your authentic self.

The Ripple Effect of Healing

Addressing unacknowledged trauma doesn't just benefit you—it can positively impact your relationships and environment. As you become more attuned to your needs and emotions, you may find that you:

- Communicate More Effectively: A clearer understanding of your feelings allows for more honest and constructive conversations.

- Build Stronger Connections: Authenticity attracts like-minded individuals and deepens existing relationships.

- Inspire Others: Your journey can encourage those around you to explore their own paths to healing.

A Self-Reflection Exercise: Take a moment for a guided reflection

1. Find a Quiet Space: Sit comfortably, close your eyes, and take a few deep breaths.

2. Scan Your Body: Notice any areas of tension or discomfort. What emotions are present?

3. Recall a Recent Emotional Reaction: Think of a time when you felt a strong emotion that seemed disproportionate to the situation.

4. Explore the Feeling: What might have triggered this response? Does it remind you of any past experiences?

5. Offer Yourself Compassion: Acknowledge that it's okay to feel this way. Place a hand over your heart if it feels comforting.

6. Set an Intention: Consider one small step you can take to support your healing, such as journaling about the experience or discussing it with someone you trust.

Moving Forward

Healing is not a linear process. There will be days of progress and days that feel more challenging. The important thing is to remain patient and kind to yourself throughout the journey.

Remember that seeking help is a sign of strength. Whether through professional support, trusted friends, or self-guided practices, you have resources available to assist you.

Closing Thoughts

As we continue our conversation, I want to remind you again that you are not alone. Many of us carry unseen burdens, and it's through acknowledging and addressing them that we find relief and empowerment.

By recognizing unacknowledged trauma, you're taking a courageous step toward greater self-awareness and fulfillment. This journey may require vulnerability, but also opens the door to profound personal growth.

I encourage you to embrace this process with an open heart, trusting that each step you take brings you closer to your authentic self.

Looking Ahead

In the next chapter, we'll explore how to redefine success on your own terms. We'll discuss strategies for aligning your life with your values and passions, moving away from external expectations toward a more personalized and fulfilling path.

Until then, give yourself grace, and know that every effort you make toward self-understanding is a valuable investment in your well-being.

Part II:
Redefining Success on Your Terms

Chapter 6

What Expectations Do You Want to Fulfill?

When was the last time you paused amid the whirlwind of daily life to ask yourself, "Whose expectations am I actually trying to meet?" It's a question that can open doors to profound self-awareness and intentional living. Too often, we find ourselves chasing goals and fulfilling roles that, upon closer examination, may not align with our true desires.

Intentional Living

Intentional living is about making conscious choices that reflect your authentic self. It's the difference between living on autopilot—reacting to life's demands—and taking the wheel to steer your life in the direction you genuinely want to go.

It's all too easy to settle into our Tripple Trap of pleasing, performing, and perfecting. After all, it has gotten us this far, right? At least, that is how our subconscious sees it. Pleasing offers a reward and may have kept us safe in life's more challenging situations. Performing, too, provides attention, what feels like acceptance, and a sense of belonging. Why would we want to stop doing what provides those things? And I don't know about you, but perfecting has delivered some of my best work!

So why would our subconscious mind allow us to stop these behaviors that have brought us at least some success and positive outcomes?

That's where intentional living comes in.

Intentional living invites us to step back and reevaluate where we invest our time and energy. It encourages us to make deliberate choices rather than defaulting to what others expect or even ourselves.

What Do You Really Want?

This is a big question, isn't it? 'What do you really want?' It can be daunting because it requires honesty and vulnerability. It may mean allowing yourself to confront some challenging questions and feelings. It might involve peeling back layers of societal conditioning, family expectations, and self-imposed pressures to uncover your true desires.

After my long break, I realized it was time to sit and ask the question again. I found it difficult at first, so I started small. I asked myself:

- What activities bring me joy?

- What work feels meaningful to me?

- What kind of relationships do I want to nurture?

- How do I want to feel on a daily basis?

To reevaluate my business, I also asked:

- Why did I start this work?

- Do I still feel connected to it?

- If I did return to this work, would the mission be the same, or would it change?

- Should I consider other paths? If so, what is the road less traveled?

- Is it time to close this chapter?

Through journaling and reflection, I began to uncover the answers. My business was based on a mission I felt I was placed on this earth to fulfill. However, I was also spreading myself too thin; sometimes, my exhaustion sapped the joy out of the mission.

Additionally, I always tried to do the things that were recommended by the pros. I had invested tens of thousands of dollars in coaches, programs, and business tools. These things can be terrific when focused and intentional. In my case, I was using these things in an attempt to gain focus, which only left my efforts fragmented and added irons to my fire. I really thought I had to do all of these things to have the success I was after. It never occurred to me that a break to reassess the journey would help me get more bang for my buck and my energy.

Sure, I had some success, but I had completely lost sight of the original mission. So much so that within a three-year span, I reinvented the business two or three times. In following these programs that questioned my niche, my goals, and my profit margin, I had jumped onto a bit of a merry-go-round.

At one point, I had two full-time jobs, working until 10 pm every night, including weekends. But the 'busy' got the best of me and I also decided to start a non-profit organization! I threw myself into it. My partner did not, so I picked up the slack. By the end of it, my body made the decision for me. I was forced to take a break. It's kind of amazing how the body talks to us, even when we refuse to listen. Now, sitting still was no longer a choice. I would be spending weeks doing so.

As I recovered and did 'the work,' I journaled about how I valued creativity, meaningful connections, and time for self-care more than the accolades or external validations I had been chasing.

So, from my own experience and the experiences of those I coach, I'd like to share with you that it's essential to permit yourself to explore your desires without judgment. Remember, there's no 'right' answer—only what's true for you.

Self-Reflection Exercise: Discovering Your True Desires

Set aside some quiet time and grab your journal. Consider the following prompts:

- Joyful Activities: List activities that make you lose track of time because you're so engaged and happy.

- Meaningful Work: Reflect on times when you felt your work made a positive impact. What were you doing?

- Ideal Day: Describe your ideal day from morning to night. What does it include? Who are you with? Write it like an incredibly detailed scene or series of scenes. Use the five senses.

- Core Feelings: Identify the feelings you want to experience regularly (e.g., peace, excitement, connection).

- Reevaluate as needed: Examine the 'why' and your journey.

- Lifestyle matters: What is the life you want for yourself? Sometimes, the thing we think will get us there isn't the thing at all. Focus instead on the desired experience as you write. There may be surprises that reveal themselves.

Write freely, without censoring yourself. This exercise is for your eyes only.

Communicating What You Want

Once you've gained clarity on your true desires, the next step is communicating them—to yourself and others. This can be challenging, especially if it involves changing established patterns or disappointing others who have certain expectations of you.

A Pause

Hold up! Gut check!

"But Charlie, I need a plan before I tell others what I want!"

No, you don't. This may feel extremely uncomfortable, but you don't yet need a plan to communicate what you want to the important people in your life. Choosing *who* you communicate your desires with is definitely reasonable and required here. But the plan will come as you settle into your desires.

Remember, communicating your wants is essential for living authentically and building relationships based on honesty.

Start with Self-Affirmation

Before expressing your desires to others, affirm them to yourself. Acknowledge that your wants are valid and important. This internal validation strengthens your confidence when sharing with others.

Communicating with Others

Here are some steps to effectively communicate what you want:

1. Choose the Right Time and Place: Find a moment when both you and the other person are calm and open to conversation.

2. Be Clear and Specific: Articulate your desires plainly. For example, "I've realized that I need more time for creative projects, so I'll be stepping back from some of my current commitments."

3. Use "I" Statements: Focus on your feelings and needs. This reduces the likelihood of the other person feeling blamed or defensive.

4. Anticipate Reactions with Compassion: Understand that others may need time to adjust. They might be surprised or have questions. Approach the conversation with empathy.

5. Stand Firm but Kind: Hold your ground respectfully. It's okay to reiterate your needs if the conversation veers off course.

Dealing with Discomfort

Communicating your wants may feel uncomfortable, especially if you're not used to asserting yourself. It's natural to feel nervous. Remember that discomfort is often a sign of growth.

If you encounter resistance or pushback, stay calm and reiterate your position. It's essential to listen to the other person's perspective, sure. But it is also critical to honor your own needs.

Overcoming Fear of Disappointment

A common barrier to communicating our desires is the fear of disappointing others. We worry about upsetting family members, friends, or colleagues. However, continually suppressing your own wants to please others can lead to resentment and burnout. It's healthier for all involved when relationships are based on honesty.

Consider this: Those who genuinely care about you will ultimately want you to be happy and fulfilled.

Embracing Intentional Choices

Intentional living is about making choices that align with your true desires. It might mean saying 'no' to opportunities that don't resonate with you, even if they seem prestigious or others expect you to accept them.

Creating a Personal Manifesto

A personal manifesto declares your intentions, desires, and values to yourself and the Universe. It serves as a guide for making decisions and staying aligned with what you truly want.

Steps to Create Your Manifesto:

1. Reflect on Your Discoveries: Use insights from your earlier reflections on what you really want.

2. Write in Affirmative Language: Phrase your statements in the positive present tense. For example, "I prioritize meaningful connections and allocate time to nurture my relationships."

3. If something you write using affirmative language doesn't yet resonate—try this language instead: "*I invite in* new, meaningful connections," or "*I invite in* opportunities to allocate my time to nurture my relationships." This language will help your subconscious lean toward belief.

4. Include Your Intentions: Clearly state how you intend to live and make choices.

5. Keep It Visible: Place your manifesto somewhere you'll see it regularly to remind yourself of your commitments.

Example Personal Manifesto:

- I live intentionally, making choices that align with my authentic self.

- I honor my desire for creativity by dedicating weekly time to artistic pursuits.

- I communicate my needs openly and respectfully, fostering honest relationships.

- I embrace opportunities that resonate with my passions and decline those that do not.

- I prioritize my well-being, recognizing that self-care enables me to give my best to others.

- *I invite in* silent reminders that I am the 'adult in the room' and take responsibility for *allowing* myself the space to put myself first.

Navigating Challenges

As you begin to live more intentionally and communicate your wants, you may face challenges:

- Internal Doubts: It's normal to question yourself. Return to your reflections and manifesto for reassurance.

- External Pressures: Others may not understand your choices. Stay grounded in your self-awareness.

- Unexpected Obstacles: Flexibility is key. Adjust your plans as needed while staying true to your core desires.

The Rewards of Authentic Living

Embracing what you truly want and communicating it effectively leads to numerous benefits:

- Increased Fulfillment: You're more likely to feel satisfied and content when your actions align with your desires.

- Stronger Relationships: Honesty fosters deeper connections based on mutual understanding.

- Personal Growth: Living intentionally encourages continuous self-discovery and development.

- Reduced Stress: Letting go of obligations that don't serve you alleviates unnecessary pressure.

Self-Reflection Exercise: Assessing Alignment

Periodically check in with yourself:

- Are my daily actions reflecting what I truly want?

- Have I communicated my desires to those affected by them?

- Am I honoring my personal manifesto?

If you find discrepancies, consider what adjustments you can make.

Closing Thoughts

Choosing which expectations you want to fulfill is a powerful step toward living a life that's authentically yours. Deviating from the path other people or situations have placed before you requires courage and change, but the journey leads to genuine fulfillment.

Remember, *it's your life*. You have the right to decide what you want and to communicate those desires openly. By doing so, you not only enrich your own experience but also inspire others to consider their own paths.

Finally, a gentle reminder here that it's okay to change your mind. The sunk cost fallacy is just that.

As we conclude our conversation, I encourage you to embrace intentional living. Take the time to discover what you really want and have the courage to communicate it. Your authentic life awaits.

In the next chapter, we'll explore "The Power of Selective Focus," where we'll discuss strategies for prioritizing what's truly important to you and how to effectively manage your commitments.

Chapter 7

The Power of Selective Focus

Are you familiar with the Eisenhower Matrix? This time-management tool helps you prioritize tasks by urgency and importance. Picture a piece of paper with two lines crossed that create four quadrants. The top-left quadrant signifies the 'urgent and important tasks.' The planning zone is the top-right quadrant, 'important, but not urgent.' The bottom two quadrants are for delegation and deletion. The Eisenhower Matrix originated from a quote by Dwight D. Eisenhower, the 34th President of the United States.

Eisenhower used the idea to prioritize tasks as a general in the US Army, Supreme Allied Commander of NATO Forces, and president. Stephen Covey, author of The 7 Habits of Highly Effective People, then popularized the concept as a task management tool.

Here's why I'm bringing this tool up: So many leaders live in the first quadrant, where *everything* seems both urgent *and* important. This makes us firefighters always concerned about putting out the fire.

The problem with firefighting is that it hijacks our amygdala, the part of the limbic system that controls emotions and behavior. It identifies threats and triggers the body's "fight or flight" response. So, if *everything* is a fire, the amygdala is always in firefighting or fire-fleeing mode.

Naturally, the subconscious does its job of protecting you, releasing epinephrine and cortisol into the bloodstream. Your heart rate increases, as does your breathing. Your blood pressure increases, and your pupils dilate. Your palms may sweat, and your face may appear flushed. Here's my favorite: It may become difficult to think clearly, or your behavior may become inappropriate or irrational. Emotions may take over thoughts.

Let me ask you: If we are *always* in firefighting mode, what is our body doing with all those stress responses? How is our mind functioning?

Fire Prevention Instead of Firefighting

For a long time, my days felt like an endless series of emergencies. I was the firefighter, rushing from one blazing issue to the next, barely catching my breath. Every task seemed urgent, every request couldn't wait, and I constantly put out fires. I congratulated myself for being so wonderfully efficient. I felt important and in charge. Between you and me, I loved those feelings. I loved being the one who solved the problems and took control. I loved that people depended on me to be the firefighter. All I was missing was my own calendar.

But seriously, why *wouldn't* I just keep on this way?

As I've said, it is incredible how the body insists on its own behalf, even when we don't want to listen. One night, I was driving down the highway, coming home from Target. This particular stretch of road is where folks tend to drive too fast, and it was the busiest time of day. Cars were whizzing past as I drove, and quite suddenly, I felt my face go flush, and there was an elephant on my chest!

I saw the ER just across the street, swerved into the parking lot, parked my car, and stood before the intake nurse within minutes.

"I... think I'm having a... heart attack..." I stammered as I tried to breathe.

Well, that did it. I was immediately rushed back, and diodes were placed all over my body as the team rushed to conduct an EKG. Another nurse wheeled in her little computer cart and began asking me questions. Within a couple of minutes, they knew I was *not* having a heart attack but, more than likely, a panic attack. They each began to make their way out of the room, and the nurse kept an eye on my heart rate, encouraging me to breathe.

Later, after they medicated me and let me rest, I thought about how ridiculous it was that I, of all people, would end up in the ER having a panic attack. I meditate, for goodness' sake!

But the chaos of my lifestyle had caught up with me, regardless of the few healthy habits I had established. Oh, my body had tried to warn me, first with headaches and then with moments that felt like little bursts of anxiousness. Do you know those? When your heart thumps loudly and your breathing quickens? When you place your hand on your chest reactively to calm yourself?

Yeah, I ignored those.

Over the next few days, I realized it was time to focus on fire *prevention* and hang up my hose.

Think about it: Firefighters don't just extinguish fires but also educate the public on fire prevention, installing smoke detectors, and conducting safety inspections. They know that preventing a fire is far better than fighting one.

I began to apply this mindset to my own life. Instead of reacting to every crisis, I started to identify potential issues before they erupted. I set aside time for planning and reflection, anticipating and addressing challenges proactively. I led discussions in meetings about things not yet on the radar and began to shift my focus out of the minutiae and over the bigger picture.

Monday mornings were always chaotic, setting a frazzled tone for the week. So, I began dedicating time on Friday afternoons to organize my tasks for the upcoming week, which also shifted my focus over the weekend away from work. This simple shift allowed me to start Mondays with a clear plan, reducing stress and increasing productivity.

Delegating and Sharing Responsibilities

One of the hardest lessons for me was learning to delegate. I used to believe that if I wanted something done right, I had to do it myself. Sound familiar? Holding onto that belief kept me overwhelmed and prevented others from stepping up. Plus, remember my admitting how much I enjoyed being the one called into action? Letting that go wasn't easy either. Recognizing how I benefitted from the habits I had formed was the first step toward letting them go.

Of course, my first instinct was to hang on to those benefits and prevent others from assisting me. After all, no one could be as good as I was at… what were those things again?

It's a bit ridiculous to me now, looking back at my inability to trust others to show up. Look, let's be honest here: The likelihood was that those things wouldn't get done as well as I did them. But I had to learn to be open to the possibility, and I had to learn to allow them to be less than perfect. Delegating isn't about offloading tasks onto others; it's about recognizing that you don't have to carry the entire burden alone. It's an opportunity to collaborate, empower others, and create space for yourself to focus on what truly requires your attention.

Choosing the things that matter most to spend time on can be an incredibly satisfying experience.

I understand that letting go of… well, anything, can be scary. You might worry that the task won't be done correctly, or you'll lose control over the outcome. It is also possible to fear *not* being the one who earns the accolades for 'doing it all.' But consider this: holding onto everything landed me in that ER.

Here's what helped me:

- Start Small: Begin by delegating minor tasks and gradually move on to more significant responsibilities.

- Set Clear Expectations: Communicate the desired outcome and any important details.

- Trust and Support: Allow others the autonomy to complete the task in their own way and be available for guidance if needed.

- Embrace Different Approaches: Recognize that different doesn't mean wrong. Others might have more effective methods, and that is okay.

Prioritization Tools: Let's revisit the Eisenhower Matrix.

This matrix helps you categorize tasks based on their urgency and importance, dividing them into four quadrants:

- Urgent and Important (Do First)

- Important but Not Urgent (Schedule)

- Urgent but Not Important (Delegate)

- Not Urgent and Not Important (Eliminate)

Briefly, I want to establish permission for you to eliminate things from your task lists. Delete those emails, say 'no,' and otherwise 'eliminate' them from your life. It's okay. Really.

How to Use the Matrix

- List Your Tasks: Write down everything you need to do.

- Categorize Each Task:

- Urgent and Important: Deadlines, crises, pressing problems.

- Important but Not Urgent: Long-term goals, planning, personal growth.

- Urgent but Not Important: Interruptions, some emails or calls.

- Not Urgent and Not Important: Distractions, time-wasters.

- Take Action:

- Do First: Handle tasks in the first quadrant promptly.

- Schedule: Allocate time for second quadrant tasks.

- Delegate: Assign third quadrant tasks to someone else.

- Eliminate: Remove fourth quadrant tasks from your list.

Applying the Matrix

Let's say you have the following tasks:

- Finalize preparations for tomorrow's presentation (Urgent and Important)

- Plan your next vacation (Important but Not Urgent)

- Respond to a non-critical email (Urgent but Not Important)

- Scroll through social media (Not Urgent and Not Important)

Using the matrix, you focus on preparing for the presentation first. You schedule time to plan your vacation, delegate or automate the email response if possible, and eliminate or limit time spent on social media.

Shifting Your Mindset

The Eisenhower Matrix isn't just a tool—it's a mindset shift. It encourages you to be intentional with your time, focusing on tasks that align with your goals and values.

I found that many of my "urgent" tasks weren't truly important. They felt pressing because they were in my immediate field of vision, but they didn't contribute significantly to my priorities.

By regularly assessing my tasks, I began to allocate more time to activities that mattered to me, like pursuing hobbies, spending quality time with loved ones, and investing in personal development.

Real-Life Application: Martina's Story

Let me introduce you to Martina, a client who struggled with feeling overwhelmed by her to-do list. She was constantly busy but felt she wasn't progressing toward her goals. Part of the problem, she later realized, was that all of her energy was spent on problem-solving urgent issues, and none of it was in the planning of her business' growth. And so, her business had seemed to plateau.

I showed Martina the Eisenhower Matrix and spoke about firefighting. The realization was that she was spending most of her time on urgent but not important activities—like attending meetings that didn't require her input or responding immediately to every email.

By delegating and setting boundaries around her availability, Martina freed up time to focus on important but not urgent tasks, such as developing that new product line she had been thinking about. This shift both reduced her stress and reignited her passion for her business.

Embracing the Power of No

An essential part of selective focus is learning to say 'no' to tasks and requests that don't serve your priorities. This doesn't mean being unhelpful or dismissive; it's about respecting your time and energy.

I used to say 'yes' to every request, fearing I'd disappoint others or miss opportunities. But constantly agreeing to everything left me stretched thin and resentful.

Here's how I learned to say 'no' gracefully:

Be Polite but Firm: "Thank you for thinking of me, but I won't be able to take that on right now."

Offer Alternatives: "I'm unavailable, but perhaps [Name] could assist you."

Set Clear Boundaries: Let others know your availability and limits.

Don't Over-Explain: A simple, honest response is sufficient.

Or, just say no without an explanation. This can be: "No, thank you." or "I'd rather not, thanks." or more simply, "No."

Remember the 'hell yes' effect. Every time you say no to one thing, you are saying 'hell yes' to another.

Creating Space for What Matters

Selective focus isn't just about managing tasks—it's about creating space for what truly matters in your life. When you clear away the non-essential, you make room for joy, creativity, and meaningful connections.

Think about the activities that nourish your soul. It could be spending time in nature, practicing a hobby, or simply relaxing without a to-do list hanging over your head. We reclaim control over our time and energy by intentionally choosing where to direct our focus.

Self-Reflection Exercise: Your Focus Audit

I invite you to conduct a 'Focus Audit':

Track Your Time: For one week, note how you spend your time daily.

- Identify Patterns: Where are you investing most of your time? Are there activities that consume time without adding value?

- Assess Alignment: Do your daily activities align with your priorities and values?

- Make Adjustments:

- Eliminate: Remove or reduce time spent on low-value tasks.

- Delegate: Identify tasks others can handle.

- Prioritize: Allocate time to important but not urgent activities.

This exercise can reveal surprising insights and help you make conscious choices about where to focus your energy.

Moving Forward Together

Shifting from a reactive to a proactive approach takes practice. Be patient with yourself as you implement these changes, and celebrate small victories along the way.

Remember, it's okay to seek support. Share your intentions with friends, family, or colleagues who can encourage you and hold you accountable.

Closing Thoughts

The power of selective focus lies in its ability to transform chaos into clarity. By preventing fires instead of constantly fighting them, delegating tasks, and prioritizing effectively, you open the door to *more*. More love, more passion, more delight, and more joy.

In our next chapter, we'll explore redefining success and how embracing quality over quantity can lead to more profound satisfaction in one's personal and professional life.

Chapter 8

Redefining Success

Have you ever chased a dream, reached the pinnacle you set for yourself, and then felt an unexpected emptiness? I have. It's a disconcerting experience when the success you've worked so hard for doesn't bring the fulfillment you anticipated.

One coach friend of mine calls it "Anticipation Letdown."

I can't tell you how many clients end up in my proverbial chair because they feel empty. Remember Grayson, shoulding all over herself? "I *should* feel happy" can just as easily read, "I feel empty."

In my experience, feeling empty is almost always the result of selling ourselves short.

So many of us spend so much time pleasing, performing, and perfecting that we never even ask what success looks like for us. Sure, we buy into other people's ideas about success, but are we taught as women to invent what our success could look like based on our desires?

Seriously.

What *is* success for *you*?

Many years ago now, my grandmother passed away from cancer. It all went so fast. At her funeral, so very many people showed up. Some folks who got up to speak were neighbors and friends, and they told stories of how this one time, Mary made us cookies, or Mary invited us in and listened to our struggles, or Mary was always so kind and generous.

Later, my grandpa found her daily calendars, all with little poems and scribbles. There were so many that they filled a family-bound book, and we each received a copy.

Years later, when my Auntie passed, it was very much the same experience for those of us left behind. I still remember a neighbor of hers standing up and telling the story of how Auntie Laurie would take their daughter to school. None of us knew.

I thought then that *this* was success.

It's been some years since, and while I do hope people laugh and share good memories of me someday, my idea of success for *myself* is different.

What Does Success Look Like For You Now?

When I was younger, success had a clear-cut definition for me. It was all about the external markers: a high-powered career, a beautiful home, and the admiration of peers. I thought I'd feel content and accomplished if I could check all those boxes.

I threw myself into my work, climbing the corporate ladder with determination. Late nights at the office, weekends spent catching up on emails, constantly being 'on'—these became my norms. My social calendar was equally packed, filled with networking events and social gatherings. I was always busy, always in motion.

On the outside, I looked successful. I had a million-dollar home, two wonderful kids, a wealthy husband, and other rich, successful people around me. We always entertained and looked the part. I had 'busy' down to a science. *Everyone* wanted what I had. I, too, told myself that I *should* be happy. For over a decade, I had done an excellent job convincing everyone that I was.

And then something shifted.

On a vacation sailing up the Croatian coast with two other couples, my narcissistic husband and I fought almost the entire trip. For the first time in our relationship, I was genuinely *over* keeping up pretenses and trying to meet his demands and expectations. After too long, I realized he just wanted me to be someone else.

I hadn't slept well that night, as we were fighting in our tiny cabin. His constant hissing, going over my many, many faults, was finally enough. I went out, sat on the deck alone, and watched the sunrise.

At that moment, I realized that whoever it was he wanted me to be—I didn't want to be her.

That moment sparked a period of deep introspection. I began to question the definition of success I'd been chasing. Was it indeed mine, or was it shaped by societal expectations and the desires of others?

Was it because I thought this life was what I *should* want?

Listening to the Inner Voice

I started to pay attention to a quiet voice inside me that I'd long ignored. It whispered about what I wanted and what, deep down, I knew I deserved. And I deserved *better*.

Fifteen years later now, I still have to quiet myself and lean in to listen to that voice.

My definition of success has changed dramatically. It is less about external validation and more about inner fulfillment. As a single woman approaching sixty—I still don't know how 'over 50' happened—the desire for safety and security has only grown. I'd be lying if I claimed otherwise. But beneath that very external validation of my 'success' is the knowledge that I'm directing my energies toward being who I am meant to be.

After decades of pleasing, performing, and perfecting, I have found my 'True North.' And as long as I continue toward that, I am already successful. Oh, I'll have to (using a sailor's term here) tack a lot, as the seas are pretty rough sometimes. But in doing that, I am a success.

Embracing Change

It's natural for our perspectives to evolve as we grow and gain new experiences. What once drove us may no longer hold the same appeal. Acknowledging this isn't a sign of failure; it's a testament to our growth.

I recently spoke with a dear friend, Alex, who shared a similar journey. Alex had been a lawyer at a prestigious firm, the culmination of years of hard work and dedication. But despite the success, he felt a persistent dissatisfaction.

Returning from a short sabbatical, Alex showed up outside my home, gave me a call, and told me to meet him outside. Looking for his car, I asked, "Where are you?"

Alex giggled, "Right in front of you."

Near my driveway was a man wearing a helmet on a BMW motorcycle. I realized that it was Alex. Later, over dinner, he explained that he was not going through a mid-life crisis but had realized on his sabbatical that he was chasing the almighty dollar rather than a quality life. He rediscovered his love of travel and his camera, and it was time to truly live again.

Now, Alex speaks of feeling alive like he never did before. His definition of success transformed from one centered on prestige and income to one rooted in passion and creativity.

Quality Over Quantity: Emphasizing Depth of Engagement

In reevaluating success, I have begun to see the value of quality over quantity. It's easy to divert our focus to accumulating achievements, experiences, and possessions. Now, I try to slow down and spend time fully savoring what matters most to me.

The Overpacked Schedule

My calendar used to be a testament to my busyness. Every hour was accounted for, and I took pride in my ability to juggle multiple commitments. But in my quest to do everything, I was missing out on truly experiencing anything.

As a woman with two businesses, it is pretty standard to be in a crowded room of summit attendees or potential networking professionals and engage in surface-level interactions, flitting from one conversation to the next without connecting with anyone. But I've spent the last year focusing on being present with the person before me. Sure, this means I'll speak to fewer people, but the connections I make will be more genuine.

Choosing Depth

This last year has brought me some professional challenges, and choosing to lean into more intimate moments with myself has been part of the journey. There have been times when I left my phone on its little stand as I continued painting a flower with my watercolor pens in a sketchbook or canceled an engagement I had bought tickets for because, upon reflection, I realized I just wanted to stay home and relax.

Prioritizing this way hasn't always been easy, but I am living more fully, and when I do choose to spend my precious time with other people, they get depth.

The Fulfillment of Deep Engagement

There's a profound satisfaction that comes from immersing yourself fully in an experience. Whether delving into a creative project, nurturing a relationship, or simply enjoying a hobby, depth brings richness to our lives.

My friend Diana exemplifies this beautifully. An avid gardener, she spends hours enriching the soil, tending to her plants, learning about each species, and nurturing them with care. It might seem like a simple pastime to some, but it's a source of immense joy and fulfillment for Diana.

She once told me, "When I'm in my garden, time stands still. I feel connected to something larger than myself." Her commitment to this single passion brings her more happiness than any number of superficial distractions could.

Applying Quality Over Quantity in Daily Life

Emphasizing depth doesn't mean we have to limit ourselves severely; it's about making conscious choices.

- In Relationships: Instead of spreading ourselves thin among numerous acquaintances, we can invest time and energy into deepening bonds with a select few. This fosters trust, understanding, and support.

- In Activities: Rather than trying to master every skill or hobby, we can focus on those that truly ignite our passion. This allows for greater mastery and enjoyment.

- In Work, concentrating on projects that align with our values and strengths can produce higher-quality results and increase our satisfaction in our professional lives.

Redefining Success Personally

Redefining success is a personal journey, and it looks different for everyone. It's about aligning our lives with what we truly value.

For me, success now encompasses:

- Authenticity: Living in a way that reflects my true self, not who I think I should be.

- Leaving work on the desk in favor of personal time. Sometimes 'good enough' is enough.

- Impact: Contributing positively to others' lives through my work and interactions.

- Growth: Continuously learning and evolving, embracing new experiences that enrich my understanding of the world.

Your Definition of Success

I encourage you to contemplate what success means to you at this point in your life and to permit yourself to redefine success in a way that resonates with your current self.

Embracing the Journey

Redefining success isn't about reaching a final destination; it's an ongoing process of self-discovery. As we grow and change, so too may our definitions of success.

Being Open to Change

It's important to remain open and flexible. What fulfills us today might not be as fulfilling in the future, and that's perfectly natural.

And always, always, give yourself grace.

Closing Thoughts

Redefining success is a deeply personal and empowering endeavor. Focusing on what truly matters to us and embracing depth over breadth can create lives rich with meaning and joy.

As we part ways in this chapter, I hope you feel inspired to reflect on your own path. Consider where you might shift your focus to align more closely with your authentic desires.

Remember, success isn't a one-size-fits-all concept. It's a tapestry woven from our unique experiences, values, and dreams. Embrace your journey, and allow yourself to define success on your own terms.

In our next chapter, we'll explore cultivating self-compassion and how embracing kindness toward ourselves can transform our lives and relationships.

Chapter 9

Becoming Unshakable

I've always been fascinated by the complexities of the human mind—the conscious, the subconscious, and the interplay between them. As I mentioned earlier, if I were to personify my subconscious, she'd be a lot like Harley Quinn. Yes, that Harley Quinn—the quirky, unpredictable, and, let's be honest, a bit unhinged character from the comics and movies. She's been through trauma, she's misunderstood, and she operates based on her own set of rules, some of which don't align with reality.

Let me explain.

Befriending Our Subconscious: Meeting Harley Quinn

Harley Quinn, originally Dr. Harleen Quinzel, was a brilliant psychologist before her life took a dramatic turn. Her descent into chaos wasn't overnight; it was a gradual process influenced by her relationship with the Joker—a master manipulator. She represents parts of ourselves shaped by experiences and traumas, parts that may not always perceive reality accurately.

In my own life, I've come to see my subconscious as a Harley Quinn figure. She's protective but can be misguided. She reacts based on past wounds, sometimes distorting the present through the lens of old pain. She doesn't always know what's true or not, but she's fiercely committed to keeping me safe—even if her methods are counterproductive.

Life's Traumas and Misperceptions

We've all faced experiences that leave a mark. Some are overt traumas; others are subtle hurts that accumulate over time. These events shape our subconscious beliefs and reactions. Like Harley, our subconscious might latch onto certain narratives to make sense of the world, even if they're not entirely accurate.

For example, if you've been betrayed in the past, your subconscious might warn you to distrust others, even when there's no evidence of ill intent. It's an overprotection mechanism that is well-intentioned but potentially harmful.

The Subconscious as a Misguided Protector

My Harley is quick to jump to conclusions, especially when she senses a threat. She's the voice that says, "They don't like you," or "You're going to fail." She's not trying to sabotage me; she's trying to shield me from disappointment or hurt. But by acting on misperceptions or outright lies, she can create more problems than she prevents.

Being the Adult in the Room

Around 95% of brain activity is considered to be subconscious, meaning that most of our mental processes happen without our conscious awareness, effectively putting our subconscious in charge most of the time. Recognizing this dynamic is the first step toward self-regulation. It's up to us to shift the internal discussion. It's about acknowledging that while my subconscious (Harley) has a voice, she doesn't *have* to be in charge. I need to be the adult in the room—the rational, compassionate presence that listens but also questions. I can actually *rewire* her autopilot responses. Easy? No. Doable with practice and patience? Yes.

Questioning the Narratives

When Harley pipes up with her dramatic proclamations, I can pause and ask:

"Is this thought based on fact or fear?"

"What evidence do I have to support or refute this belief?"

"Am I reacting to the present moment or to something from my past?"

This process isn't about silencing my subconscious but engaging with it. It's like sitting down with Harley and saying, "I hear you. Let's look at this together."

Practicing Self-Regulation

Self-regulation is the ability to manage our thoughts, emotions, and behaviors in a way that aligns with our values and long-term goals. It's not about suppressing feelings but about responding rather than reacting.

Strategies for Self-Regulation:

- Mindfulness Meditation: This practice helps create space between stimulus and response. By observing thoughts without judgment, we can choose how to act.

- Cognitive Reframing: Challenging negative or distorted thoughts and replacing them with more balanced perspectives.

- Emotional Awareness: Recognizing and naming emotions as they arise which can reduce their intensity.

- Breathing Techniques: Deep, intentional breaths can calm the nervous system during moments of stress.

The more these strategies are practiced, the more they can become automatic.

A Tense Moment with a Colleague

Let me share a real-life example of how my inner Harley tried to take the reins and how I navigated the situation.

At a previous job, I worked closely with a colleague named Lisa. From the moment we met, I sensed tension. She was curt in meetings, often dismissed my ideas, and seemed to undermine me whenever possible. I tried to build a rapport, but my efforts were met with indifference or subtle hostility.

One afternoon, Lisa approached me and said, "Just so you know, our supervisor didn't even want to work with you on this project. She thinks you talk too much, and she prefers brevity." The words hit me like a punch to the gut. My heart raced, and a mix of anger and fear welled up inside me.

Harley's Reaction

Immediately, Harley jumped into action:

"See? They don't like you. You need to fix this! It's just like Chris always said: You talk too much!"

"You're going to lose your job if you don't change."

"This witch is trying to get you fired."

"You can't change who you are, so you might as well give up now."

"Maybe things will improve if you work harder and keep your head down."

I spent weeks afterward trying to adjust my behavior. I overanalyzed every interaction with my supervisor, second-guessed my contributions in meetings, and even considered whether I should look for a new job. The stress was overwhelming.

Questioning the Narrative

One evening, exhausted and frustrated, I decided to step back and assess the situation objectively.

"Do I have any direct feedback from my supervisor indicating she's unhappy with my work?" No. In fact, she had recently praised my performance during a team meeting.

"Could Lisa have her own motivations for telling me this?" Possibly. I'd noticed she often sought recognition and might feel threatened by my contributions.

"Am I reacting based on facts or assumptions?" Mostly assumptions fueled by my insecurities.

"Does this trigger any old stories?" Yep. Lots of them.

Taking Back Control

Armed with this clarity, I made a plan:

- Set Up a Meeting with My Supervisor: I decided to address the issue directly, seeking honest feedback.

- Prepare for the Conversation: I listed my recent accomplishments and contributions to discuss if needed.

- Manage My Emotions: I practiced deep breathing before the meeting to stay calm and centered.

The Conversation

When I met with my supervisor, I approached the topic openly:

"I've been reflecting on my work and wanted to check in with you. Do you have any feedback on how I contribute to the team?"

She looked surprised. "Actually, I've been meaning to tell you how much I appreciate your initiative on the recent project. Your insights have been valuable."

Relieved, I gently probed further. "I heard that there might be concerns about my teamwork. Is there anything I should be aware of?"

She frowned. "Not at all. Where is this coming from?"

I mentioned my conversation with Lisa without assigning blame. My supervisor sighed and shared that there had been some team dynamics issues but assured me that she valued my contributions.

Reframing the Situation

Leaving the meeting, I felt a weight lift off my shoulders. Harley had been spinning a narrative based on fear and misperception. By stepping into the adult role—questioning and seeking facts—I regained control.

I also recognized that Lisa's actions were likely driven by her insecurities. While that didn't excuse her behavior, it allowed me to approach future interactions with some understanding rather than animosity.

Building Resilience

This experience reinforced the importance of resilience—the ability to bounce back from challenges and adapt positively.

Key Components of Resilience:

- Emotional Awareness: Understanding what we're feeling and why.

- Optimism: Maintaining a hopeful outlook, even in difficult situations.

- Flexibility: Being open to new perspectives and willing to adjust our approach.

- Support Systems: Leaning on friends, family, or mentors for guidance and encouragement.

Tips for Becoming Unshakable

1. Cultivate Self-Awareness: Regularly check in with yourself. Journaling can be a helpful tool for processing thoughts and emotions.

2. Challenge Negative Thoughts: When you notice self-defeating beliefs, question their validity and seek evidence before accepting them as truth.

3. Practice Mindfulness: Engage in activities that keep you grounded in the present moment, such as meditation, yoga, or mindful breathing.

4. Set Healthy Boundaries: Protect your energy by setting limits with people who drain or negatively impact you.

5. Focus on What You Can Control: Let go of trying to manage others' opinions or actions. Concentrate on your responses and choices.

6. Develop a Support Network: Surround yourself with people who uplift and support you. Share your experiences and listen to theirs.

7. Embrace Growth Opportunities: View challenges as chances to learn and grow rather than insurmountable obstacles.

Closing Thoughts

Becoming unshakable doesn't mean we're impervious to life's difficulties. It means we develop the strength and skills to navigate them without losing our sense of self.

By befriending our subconscious—acknowledging its role but not letting it dominate—we can make more grounded decisions. We become the adults in the room, guiding ourselves with compassion and wisdom.

Remember, it's okay to have moments of doubt or fear. What's important is how we respond. By practicing self-regulation and resilience, we empower ourselves to face challenges with confidence.

As you continue on your journey, know that you're not alone. We all have our inner Harleys, but we also have the capacity to guide ourselves toward clarity and peace.

In the next chapter, we'll explore "Overcoming the Fear of Letting Go." We'll delve into the challenges of relinquishing control, trusting others, and prioritizing what truly matters. Together, we'll uncover strategies to navigate these fears and embrace a more balanced, fulfilling life.

Chapter 10

Overcoming the Fear of Letting Go

This chapter is going to be intentionally short. We've talked about this topic already, and almost all of us sigh when it comes up. It's not that we feel it isn't a legitimate issue, but that we already know we need to do some work in this area. That said, I think drawing some connections is important here.

Maintaining control is essential for those of us with Driven Woman Syndrome. If you've been challenged by this need, know you are with your people here. Many of us hold the deep-seated belief that relinquishing control is a sign of weakness or invites chaos into our lives. Let's journey together to explore where this fear originates and how we can begin to let go, allowing others to step in and support us.

The Roots of Our Need for Control

Our desire for control often stems from past traumatic experiences or the cultural narratives we've internalized. Perhaps, like me, you witnessed someone close to you lose control in a frightening or harmful way. Maybe a parent struggled with addiction, or a caregiver was unpredictable in their emotions. Simply observing these situations can instill a belief that maintaining strict control is the only way to ensure safety and stability.

In some cases, we were taught—explicitly or implicitly—that showing vulnerability or weakness was unacceptable. Even mundane expressions like "Don't let them see you sweat," "Pull up your bootstraps," or "Suck it up" reinforce the idea that any display of emotion is a flaw. Especially for women, the pressure to appear composed at all times can be immense.

The Cultural Expectations Placed on Women

Society has long grappled with stereotypes about women's emotions and capabilities. There's a pervasive myth that female leaders are too emotional to make rational decisions or that they might 'lose it' under pressure. These stereotypes are unfair and damaging, as they can limit opportunities and stifle voices that need to be heard.

We might have been encouraged to stay 'small,' to go 'unnoticed,' or to 'stay out of the way' and let others handle the 'messy' or 'complicated' stuff. These messages can be subtle—a raised eyebrow when we speak up passionately—or overt, like being told outright that we're overreacting.

Consider how often assertive women are labeled as 'bossy' or 'difficult,' while their male counterparts exhibiting the same behaviors are seen as strong leaders. This double standard can make us hesitant to express ourselves fully or to relinquish control for fear of being judged harshly, even by each other.

The Weaponization of "Crazy"

There's a troubling tactic used far too often in our society when someone decides they want a strong, opinionated woman to be quiet: they simply label her as 'crazy.' This dismissive and derogatory term undermines credibility and silences dissent.

Think about high-profile women who have been subjected to this label when they've challenged the status quo or spoken out against injustices. In personal relationships, too, expressing legitimate concerns can be met with accusations of being 'irrational' or 'hysterical.'

By branding women as 'crazy,' the focus shifts from the content of their message to an attack on their character. It's a way to disempower and control.

Reflecting on Our Own Experiences

While we won't delve into personal stories here, let's pause to consider where we've seen or experienced this phenomenon:

- In the Workplace: Have you ever hesitated to share an idea in a meeting because you feared being dismissed or ridiculed?

- In Relationships: Have your feelings or concerns been minimized by being told you overreacted?

- In Media and Culture: How often are strong female characters portrayed as unstable or erratic?

Ask yourself: Has the fear of being labeled or judged ever held me back from letting go or expressing myself honestly?

The Illusion of Control as a Shield

Holding onto control can feel like a safeguard against these judgments. If we manage every detail, keep our emotions in check, and avoid vulnerability, perhaps we can prevent others from calling us 'unstable' or 'unhinged.'

But this constant vigilance is exhausting and ultimately unsustainable. It can also prevent us from forming deep connections and experiencing the support that comes from trusting others.

Reframing Control

Let's explore the idea that being 'out of control' doesn't necessarily mean chaos or weakness. Not having all the control can be liberating and empowering.

- Empowering Others: When we relinquish some control, we allow others to step up, contribute, and shine. This can strengthen relationships and foster collaboration.

- Reducing Stress: Carrying the weight of everything is heavy. Letting go lightens our load and can improve our mental and emotional well-being.

- Encouraging Growth: Embracing vulnerability allows us to learn and grow. It opens the door to new experiences and perspectives.

Trusting Those Around Us

Insisting on always having control can inadvertently convey that we don't trust the people around us. It can create distance and hinder the development of mutual respect and understanding. Worse, it can build walls around us that we don't even know are there.

Sometimes, the message received can be "I don't need you."

We can build more meaningful relationships by allowing others to help and support us, but that doesn't mean we must eliminate our protective layers and allow injury. Starting with baby steps is key here. Just learning to let go of *some* of the things we are in control of can foster trust.

Practical Steps to Let Go and Trust Others

- Identify Areas Where You Can Relinquish Control

- Start small. Choose a task or responsibility that you typically handle and consider delegating it. This might be allowing a colleague to lead a meeting or letting a family member plan a social event.

- Communicate Openly

- Share your intentions with those involved. Let them know you trust them and are interested in collaborating more closely. Open communication can alleviate misunderstandings and set clear expectations.

- Embrace Imperfection

- Recognize that others might approach tasks differently than you would. That's okay. Focus on the outcome rather than micro-managing the process. Mistakes may happen, but they are opportunities for learning and growth.

- Practice Patience

- Letting go of control won't happen overnight. Be patient with yourself and others as you adjust to new dynamics.

- Reflect on the Experience

- After taking steps to relinquish control, take time to reflect. How did it feel? What went well? What challenges arose? Use these insights to guide future efforts.

Prioritizing What Truly Matters

Letting go doesn't mean abandoning all control. It's about being intentional with where you direct your energy and focus.

By clarifying what's truly important, you can maintain control over these aspects while trusting others with less critical areas or where their strengths complement yours.

Allowing Others to Support Us

When we let go of the need for perfection and control in every area, we create space for others to contribute. This eases our burden and enriches our lives through shared experiences and diverse perspectives.

Self-Reflection Exercise: The Letting Go Inventory

Let's put these ideas into practice with a reflective exercise.

Step 1: Identify Areas of Control

Make a List: Write down all the areas in your life where you feel the need to maintain control. This could include work projects, household tasks, social planning, etc.

Step 2: Evaluate the Necessity of Control

- Assess Importance: For each item, ask yourself:

- Is my control in this area necessary?

- Does it align with my core values and priorities?

- What would happen if I let go or shared control?

Step 3: Determine Potential for Delegation or Sharing

- Identify Opportunities: Highlight items where you could delegate or share responsibilities. Consider who could assist and how this might benefit both of you.

- Automation is another form of delegation. What can you automate?

Step 4: Plan to Let Go

- Set Intentions: Choose one or two areas to focus on initially.

- Communicate: Have conversations with those involved to express your intentions and establish a collaborative approach.

- Set Realistic Expectations. Understand that everyone is learning. Be open to adjustments along the way.

Step 5: Reflect and Adjust

- Monitor Your Feelings: Pay attention to how letting go affects your stress levels, relationships, and overall well-being.

- Celebrate Successes: Acknowledge positive outcomes and growth.

- Learn from Challenges: If difficulties arise, consider what can be learned and how to navigate them moving forward.

Closing Thoughts

Overcoming the fear of letting go is a courageous step toward a more balanced and fulfilling life. It requires challenging long-held beliefs and societal narratives that have shaped our perceptions of control and vulnerability.

By trusting others and prioritizing what truly matters, we not only ease our burdens but also foster stronger connections and empower those around us.

Remember, letting go doesn't mean losing control; it means choosing where to invest your energy and allowing others to share the journey with you.

As we move forward, let's embrace the possibilities of releasing the tight grip we've held. Together, we can create a more supportive, collaborative, and enriching environment for ourselves and those we interact with.

In our next chapter, we'll delve into 'Building a Life Aligned with Your Values.' We'll explore how to identify what you truly stand for, let go of external validation, and create a personal success statement that reflects your priorities and goals.

Part III:
Embracing Brave Greatness

Chapter 11

Building a Life Aligned with Your Values

"Those who stand for nothing fall for anything." — Alexander Hamilton

This quote has always resonated deeply with me. It's a stark reminder that without a clear understanding of our values, we can easily be swayed by external influences and lose sight of who we truly are.

Inheriting Values from Our Culturescape

Most of us grow up inheriting our parents' values and those of our culture—the "culturescape" we're immersed in from birth. By the age of seven, we've already been taught what to believe, how to behave, and what's important. These early lessons form the foundation of our value system, often without us even realizing it.

We rarely question these inherited values, gliding through life on autopilot. But have you ever stopped to consider what those values are? Do you have your values written down anywhere? Are there any you've outgrown? Are there new ones you'd like to embrace? Do you carry values from negative experiences that never served you and should, therefore, be released?

A Personal Journey Through Inherited Values

Growing up, I absorbed a myriad of values from my family. My parents and grandparents instilled in me the importance of questioning authority—a trait that encouraged critical thinking and independence. The holiday table was often the setting for lively discussions about politics, history, and current events. Being well-read wasn't just encouraged; it was expected. Books were my refuge, and library visits were a cherished weekly ritual.

Education was highly valued. Being the first in my family to graduate from college wasn't just a personal goal; it was a collective aspiration, symbolizing progress and opportunity. My grandmother often spoke of the pride of being valedictorian in grade school. While not terribly exciting for some, as a Mexican immigrant who came to the United States as a young girl, it was a very big deal. Her pride in speaking perfect American English was a cornerstone in my house of values. By the age of nine, I knew I would be a teacher and a writer, striving to be a curious, determined individual who valued knowledge and dialogue.

However, alongside these positive values, I picked up others that didn't serve me as well. There were unspoken rules about keeping emotions tightly controlled and a tendency to avoid vulnerability. Traumatic experiences added values as well. And while these traits were meant to protect, they often left me feeling isolated and disconnected from my own feelings.

Questioning and Designing My Values

As I navigated my late forties, I realized that some of my inherited values no longer fit the person I was becoming. This realization coincided with my work on understanding and befriending my subconscious—my inner Harley Quinn. I recognized that to work harmoniously with my subconscious, I needed to consciously define my values.

1. Seeking Inspiration Through Quotes and Literature

As a former high school English teacher, I've always found solace and wisdom in words. I began by searching for quotes that resonated with me, collecting snippets of wisdom from authors, historical figures, and even fictional characters.

Characters from literature, especially those from the Laura Ingalls Wilder series I adored as a child, greatly influenced my perception of 'good' values. Pa's sense of right and wrong and Laura's resilience, kindness, and adventurous spirit were still qualities I admired and wanted to embody.

I filled pages with quotes like:

"The real things haven't changed. It is still best to be honest and truthful; to make the most of what we have; to be happy with simple pleasures; and have courage when things go wrong." — Laura Ingalls Wilder

"The future belongs to those who believe in the beauty of their dreams." — Eleanor Roosevelt

"My integrity matters. My actions and values stay the same whether in front of others or to an audience of one." — Me

"I would rather have a few extraordinary friendships that enhance my life; the sort that I enjoy and trust sharing my life's journey with, mutually enriched and inspired." — Also Me

These words became touchstones, reflecting ideals I aspired to live by.

2. Journaling Across Life's Key Areas

Next, I outlined several key areas of my life:

- My Character

- My Health & Fitness

- My Spiritual and Emotional Life

- My Intellectual Life

- My Relationships & Social Life

- My Career & Financial Life

- My Quality of Life

- My Life Vision

I dedicated time to journaling about each area, reflecting on where I was and wanted to be. I asked myself questions like:

- Who do I want to be in this area of my life?

- How do I want to show up for myself and others?

- What brings me joy and fulfillment here?

- Are there any limiting beliefs or values I need to release?

This process was both enlightening and therapeutic. It allowed me to articulate my desires and acknowledge the gaps between my current reality and my aspirations.

3. Highlighting Insights and Resonant Themes

After pouring my thoughts onto the pages, I revisited my entries with a highlighter. I looked for recurring themes, powerful phrases, and quotes or attributes that stood out. Patterns began to emerge.

In my reflections on character, words like 'integrity,' 'authenticity,' and 'courage' appeared frequently. In writing about relationships, I emphasized 'trust,' 'mutual growth,' 'loyalty,' and 'deep connection.' These highlights became the building blocks of my values.

4. Crafting Maxims for Life

With these insights, I began to craft a series of maxims—a set of guiding principles that encapsulated how I wanted to live my life. These weren't just lofty ideals but actionable statements I could embody daily.

Some of the maxims I developed included:

"My integrity matters. My actions and values stay the same whether in front of others or when I'm alone."

"I prioritize my health, nurturing my body and mind to live vibrantly."

"I would rather have a few extraordinary friendships that enhance my life, the kind that enrich, inspire, and pull me forward."

These maxims could be a personal compass, directing my decisions and actions.

5. Editing and Finalizing My Personal Value Statements

Finally, I refined these maxims into clear, concise value statements. I wanted them to be memorable and impactful—a reflection of my true self.

Here are a few of the finalized statements:

Integrity: "I live authentically, ensuring that my actions align with my words and values."

Health: "I honor my body and mind by making choices that promote well-being and vitality."

Relationships: "I invite in, deep, meaningful connections that nurture mutual growth and joy."

I compiled these statements into a "Values Book," a personal manifesto of sorts. Revisiting it at least once a year allows me to reflect on my journey, celebrate progress, and make adjustments as needed.

Letting Go of External Validation

One of the most liberating aspects of defining my values was releasing the need for external validation. For much of my life, I sought approval from others—family, friends, colleagues—often molding myself to fit their expectations.

However, aligning with my values meant my sense of worth came from within. I no longer needed others to affirm my choices because they were rooted in what I genuinely believed and valued.

This shift wasn't instantaneous. It required a conscious effort to recognize when I was seeking external approval and to gently redirect my focus inward. It is *still* an area of growth for me.

Strategies to Detach from Others' Expectations

- Self-awareness: I noticed moments when I felt the urge to seek validation. Journaling helped me identify triggers and patterns.

- Mindfulness Practices: Meditation and mindfulness exercises kept me grounded in the present moment, reducing the influence of external noise.

- Affirmations: I created affirmations that reinforced my self-worth and commitment to my values, such as "I trust myself to make decisions that honor who I really am."

- Setting Boundaries: Learning to say 'no' when requests or expectations didn't align with my values was empowering and freed up energy for what truly mattered to me.

Creating a Personal Success Statement

With my values clearly defined, I wanted to articulate what success meant to me—not by society's standards, but by my own.

I reflected on the question: "What does a fulfilling, successful life look like for me?"

Combining my values and vision, I wrote:

"To me, success means living boldly and authentically, nurturing my well-being, forging deep relationships, embracing lifelong learning, making a positive impact on the world, and building a legacy of hope for women who follow."

This statement has become a touchstone, guiding my choices and reminding me of what truly matters.

Self-Reflection Exercise: Defining Your Values and Success Statement

I'd like to invite you to embark on your own journey of self-discovery. Here's a step-by-step matrix to help you define your values and create a personal success statement.

The True North Matrix

Step 1: Seek Inspiration

- Collect Quotes and Ideas: Find quotes, passages, or characters from literature, movies, or history that resonate with you.

- Reflect on Why They Resonate: Consider what these selections reveal about what you value.

Step 2: Journal Across Key Life Areas

Write about some or all of the following categories:

- My Character

- My Health & Fitness

- My Spiritual and Emotional Life

- My Intellectual Life

- My Relationships & Social Life

- My Career & Financial Life

- My Quality of Life

- My Life Vision

In your journal, explore questions like:

- What qualities do I admire in myself and others?

- How do I want to feel in this area of my life?

- What are my aspirations and goals?

- Are there beliefs or values I need to release or embrace?

Step 3: Identify Key Themes and Insights

- Review Your Entries: Highlight recurring themes, powerful words, and quotes or ideas that stand out.

- List Core Values: From your highlights, compile a list of values that are important to you.

Step 4: Create Your Maxims

- Craft Statements: Turn your core values into actionable maxims or principles.

- Be Specific and Personal: Ensure each maxim reflects your unique perspective and aspirations.

Step 5: Write Your 'True North' Success Statement

- Define Success on Your Terms: Reflect on what a successful life means to you, considering your values and maxims.

- Write a Statement: Articulate your definition of success in a concise, inspiring way.

Step 6: Compile and Reflect

- Create Your Values Book: Assemble your values, maxims, and success statement in a format that's meaningful to you. For example, mine is in a binder, and many pages resemble a vision board, with clipart words and drawings of images that support the writing.

- Print your True North Success Statement and put it where you can see it.

- Revisit Regularly: Schedule time to review and reflect on your values, updating them as you grow and evolve.

If you're not into arts and crafts projects and your 'values book' is a stack of napkins, that's fine! But put them in a special box and frame the one with your True North Success Statement on it. [D83D?][DE42?]

Embracing Your Authentic Life

Building a life aligned with your values is a deeply personal and empowering process. It requires introspection, honesty, and the courage to let go of external expectations.

By defining what you stand for, you create a solid foundation that guides your decisions and actions. This alignment brings a sense of peace and fulfillment that's unattainable when living by someone else's script.

Remember, this is *your* journey. It's okay if your values evolve over time. The key is to remain true to yourself and open to growth.

Closing Thoughts

As we conclude this chapter, I encourage you to take the time to explore and define your values. Embrace the process with curiosity and compassion. Let go of the need for external validation and trust that you have the wisdom within to create a life that reflects who you truly are.

Your values are the compass that will guide you through the complexities of life, helping you navigate challenges and seize opportunities that align with your authentic self.

In our next chapter, we'll delve into 'Leading by Example.' We'll explore how to focus on impactful work, apply selective focus in leadership roles, and build your legacy.

Chapter 12

Leading by Example

Being a parent and a leader are two of the most rewarding roles, yet they come with immense challenges. One of the most complex parts of these roles is resisting the urge to step in and shield those we care about from pain, mistakes, or wasted time. It's so tempting to intervene, offer our wisdom, and guide them away from the pitfalls looming ahead.

I remember countless times watching my children grapple with decisions or struggles, every fiber of my being wanting to swoop in and fix things for them. Shit, it still happens. Similarly, in leadership roles, I've felt the pull to direct my team away from choices I believed would lead to failure or hardship. The instinct to protect is strong, but I've learned that there's a delicate balance between guidance and overstepping.

The Pain of Letting Go

It's incredibly painful to stand by and allow nature to take its course. We often believe that all would be well if they would just listen and adhere to our sage advice. We could spare them heartache, disappointment, and setbacks. But here's the thing: that's not how *we* learned, right?

Reflecting on my own journey, I realize that many of my most profound lessons came from my mistakes and the challenges I faced head-on. Those experiences shaped me, taught me resilience, and helped me grow. By intervening too much, we might inadvertently rob others of those valuable growth and learning opportunities.

Accepting the Truth: We Can Only Change Ourselves

The uncomfortable truth is that the only person we can change is ourselves. We can't control others' actions, decisions, or paths. We can model the behavior and values we hope to inspire in others. This realization brings us to a new golden rule: Lead by example.

Leading by example isn't easy. Knowing that others might look to us as models puts tremendous pressure on us. It requires authenticity, vulnerability, and a commitment to living our values, even when it's hard.

Living Authentically and Sharing Our Journey

All we can truly do is be ourselves—live authentically, share our mistakes and successes, and hope that some wisdom may be gleaned from them. It's about showing up fully, embracing our imperfections, and demonstrating how we navigate life's ups and downs.

Fearing the Lessons I Taught

Being a woman who's made her fair share of mistakes, I've often worried about the example I set for my children. I feared that the only lessons I taught them were what *not* to do. I fretted over my daughter someday wasting years of her life pleasing, performing, and perfecting, just as I had. I feared she'd end up in abusive relationships, repeating patterns that took me years to break free from. Like I said, it's a lot of pressure.

These fears weighed heavily on me. I questioned whether I was doing enough and whether my struggles would negatively impact her. It wasn't until I had an open and honest conversation with her that I began to see things differently.

An Unexpected Perspective

One evening, over a quiet dinner, I mustered the courage to talk to my daughter about my feelings. I shared my fears, my regrets, and my hopes for her. What she said in response was incredibly kind and enlightening.

She told me that she always saw my strength—that witnessing what it took for me to leave unhealthy relationships and start over, more than once, taught her the importance of valuing oneself. She said, "Mom, you've shown me that no matter how hard things get, it's possible to choose yourself and rebuild. I'm proud of your accomplishments and hope to live up to that example."

Her words brought tears to my eyes. In all my worrying, I hadn't considered that my struggles and how I faced them could be a source of inspiration rather than a burden. It was a poignant reminder that leading by example doesn't mean being perfect; it means being authentic.

Focusing on Impactful Work

In both parenting and leadership, focusing on impactful work means prioritizing actions that align with our values and have meaningful outcomes. It's about choosing quality over quantity and investing our energy where it can make a real difference.

At Home

With my children, I am proud that regardless of any failings, the most impactful thing I did was to communicate honestly with them. Instead of trying to fake perfection or prevent every mistake, I focused on creating a safe space for them to discuss what it's like to fail and learn. Sure, I spent lots of time offering them my perspective, but I also told them I knew they would make mistakes, just like I had done.

At twelve, they both got roughly the same lecture: I was aware they would make some decisions on their own at school that I would never know about. I let them both know I trusted they would do the right thing. I hoped they would talk to me and allow me the opportunity to offer advice, mostly because I wouldn't be able to help myself.

I would love to say I then handled everything correctly. Of course, I didn't. But they always knew they had room to make their own mistakes along the way.

I had a rude awakening when, as an adult, my daughter confessed she could relate to Rapunzel in the Disney animated film Tangled. I swear, I think I heard my jaw hit the floor. But upon reflection, as a Gen-X mom, I did the thing so many of us have done: I overprotected her. While she did have room to make some decisions at school, I never allowed her to walk back and forth from school. I was pretty nosey about who her friends were, and those kids spent a lot of time in my home. She even went to high school, where I was a teacher! How much freedom can one have when they know the other kids will narc to their mom at school? So, I suppose she had a point.

In the Workplace

As a leader, I have learned to avoid micromanaging my team. I still struggle to delegate efficiently, but I do delegate. Anyone working with me knows I trust their abilities and encourage them to take ownership of their projects.

I have to confess, though, that this is still an area where I have room for improvement. My autopilot is still to take on *all the things*.

I practice a little mantra: Charlie, don't make their problems your problems.

Building a Legacy

Leading by example isn't just about the immediate impact; it's about building a legacy beyond our direct influence. It's the ripple effect of our actions and how they inspire others to carry forward our values.

Creating Positive Ripples

Every time we choose integrity over convenience, kindness over indifference, or courage over comfort, we set a precedent. Others notice, and it can inspire them to make similar choices. Over time, these small actions contribute to a larger culture of positivity and growth.

Mentoring and Sharing Wisdom

Maybe because I am a former teacher, I believe strongly in mentoring others, sharing my successes and lessons learned from failures. By being open about my journey, I hope to provide a roadmap for others navigating similar paths.

This book exemplifies my desire to live that principle as I move forward.

Integrated Leadership

Integrated leadership is the practice of harmonizing our inner values, beliefs, and goals across all facets of life—so that leadership is not compartmentalized but authentic and cohesive. This approach assumes that our personal and professional selves are interconnected, and when aligned, they empower us to lead with consistency, resilience, and clarity wherever we are.

At its core, integrated leadership is about self-awareness and alignment. Understanding our values, motivations, and purpose creates a foundation for leadership that resonates deeply with others. Rather than donning different 'masks' in various settings—such as being caring at home but rigid at work—integrated leadership fosters a unified approach to decision-making, communication, and conflict resolution.

Here's how integrated leadership manifests across key areas:

Values-Driven Decision-Making: Integrated leaders make decisions rooted in their core values rather than external expectations or isolated priorities. This can mean ensuring that career choices align with personal beliefs or fostering a work culture that reflects one's principles. This clarity helps leaders feel fulfilled and centered while also building trust and credibility with those they lead.

Authenticity and Vulnerability: Integrated leadership embraces vulnerability and transparency as strengths. Leaders who integrate personal and professional selves are more comfortable acknowledging challenges and setbacks, modeling resilience, and inviting others to do the same. This openness fosters genuine connections and encourages others to bring their whole selves to work, creating a culture of trust and respect.

Boundaries with Balance: Integration doesn't mean work and personal lives blur into each other without limits; instead, it emphasizes a healthy balance and clear boundaries. For instance, integrated leaders understand when to prioritize family, personal time, or self-care without guilt, knowing that a balanced approach sustains them in all roles. They lead by example, showing that well-being is personal and essential to organizational health.

Continuous Growth and Learning: Integrated leaders view growth as a holistic endeavor involving professional development alongside personal introspection. This can include practicing mindfulness, developing emotional intelligence, embracing lifelong learning, and reinforcing leadership skills applicable to every area of life. Integrated leaders are curious, adaptable, and open to change, nurturing a constantly evolving mindset.

Servant Leadership and Purpose-Driven Impact: Integrated leadership is also about connecting to a larger purpose that transcends any one role. This purpose might be leaving a legacy, contributing to a community, or supporting a cause. By aligning actions with a sense of purpose, integrated leaders inspire those around them to work toward meaningful goals, uniting personal fulfillment with organizational impact.

In essence, integrated leadership is about leading from a place of wholeness and alignment, ensuring that our values and purpose shine through in all areas of our lives. This model not only nurtures personal fulfillment and integrity but fosters environments where others feel empowered to lead with authenticity as well. It's a shift from managing segmented roles to embodying a cohesive and enduring approach to leadership that resonates well beyond the boardroom.

Authenticity in Leadership

When we lead authentically, we bring our whole selves to the table. This authenticity fosters trust and creates a more cohesive and supportive environment.

Balancing Roles

Balancing the roles of parent, leader, friend, and individual requires self-awareness and intentionality. It means setting boundaries, prioritizing self-care, and being mindful of allocating our time and energy.

Avoiding Burnout

Leading by example also means demonstrating healthy habits and self-care practices to avoid burnout.

Caring for Ourselves

It's essential to model self-care, showing that it's acceptable but necessary to rest, recharge, and tend to our well-being. This might include:

- Setting boundaries: Say no when necessary and protect personal time.

- Practicing Mindfulness: Engaging in activities that promote mental and emotional balance.

- Seeking Support: Recognizing when we need help and reaching out to others.

Encouraging Others to Do the Same

By caring for ourselves, we permit others to do the same. It creates a culture where well-being is valued and burnout is addressed proactively.

Self-Reflection Exercise: Embracing Authentic Leadership

I invite you to reflect on your own experiences with leading by example.

Step 1: Identify Your Core Values in Chapter 11

- Write down the values that are most important to you.

- Consider how these values manifest in your daily life.

Step 2: Reflect on Your Actions

- Think about recent situations where you led by example.

- How did your actions align with your values?

- Were there times when you struggled to embody these values? Why?

Step 3: Recognize the Impact

- Consider how your actions may have influenced others.

- Have you received feedback or observed changes that indicate your example made a difference?

Step 4: Plan for Growth

- Identify areas where you can strengthen your example.

- Set intentions for how you will embody your values moving forward.

Closing Thoughts

Leading by example is both a privilege and a responsibility. It's about being authentic, embracing our imperfections, and continuously striving to align with our values. While we cannot control others, we can influence them through our actions and how we show up in the world.

Remember, it's not about being perfect—it's about being *authentic*. Sharing our struggles and triumphs allows others to see that growth is a journey, not a destination.

As we continue on this path, let's support one another in leading lives that are true to who we are and inspire others to do the same.

In our next chapter, we'll explore 'Creating a Sisterhood.' We'll discuss the importance of building supportive communities, how we are built for connection, and ways to start or join groups that enrich our lives.

Chapter 13

Creating a Sisterhood

There's something profoundly innate about the way women connect. If we journey back to when humans first sought shelter in caves, we find evidence of a sisterhood essential for survival. Women gathered not just in proximity but in purpose. We raised our children together, shared the responsibilities of daily life, and supported each other through the trials and tribulations that came our way.

Imagine a time when the success of the community depended on cooperation. Women practiced medicine using the herbs and remedies passed down through generations. We cultivated crops, ensuring our families were nourished. We crafted clothing and goods, each stitch woven with care and intention. Our roles were diverse and vital, and we relied on one another to thrive.

This wasn't just about survival—it was about connection. The sisterhood was a sacred bond, a network of support that empowered each member. We shared stories, wisdom, and laughter around the fire. We mourned losses together and celebrated joys with equal fervor. In many cultures, this collective female strength was honored and revered.

The Isolation of Modern Times

Fast-forward to today, and the landscape looks markedly different. Technological advances and shifts in cultural norms have paradoxically connected *and* isolated us. While we can communicate with someone halfway across the world in an instant, we often don't know our neighbor's name. The communal spaces where women once gathered have diminished, replaced by individual pursuits and virtual interactions.

Globally, the narrative around powerful women has been fraught with tension. In some places, a woman with influence is seen as something to be feared, hidden away, or even extinguished. This suppression isn't just historical—it's a present reality in many parts of the world.

We tap into a formidable power when women unite to support and uplift one another. It's no wonder such unity has been resisted by those who fear change or loss of control. But it's precisely this coming together that can drive progress, foster innovation, and create meaningful change.

The Culture of Tearing Each Other Down

Unfortunately, we've often been pitted against one another instead of harnessing this collective strength. Our culture has sometimes shifted towards tearing each other down rather than building each other up. Like vultures picking at the vulnerabilities of others, we may find ourselves engaging in gossip, judgment, or competition.

These behaviors aren't new—they've been perpetuated for generations—but the rise of social media has amplified them exponentially. Behind the anonymity of screens and keyboards, some feel emboldened to hurl insults and criticisms they would never voice in person. The digital landscape can become a battleground of comparison and negativity, eroding the sense of community we deeply need.

Scrolling through social media one evening, I encountered a heated exchange between two women in a professional group. What started as a difference of opinion escalated into personal attacks and public shaming. Reading their words, I felt a pang of sadness. How did we get here? When did tearing each other down become so... acceptable?

The Shift Towards Reconnection

But amid this backdrop of division, there's a stirring—a shift in energy that's hard to ignore. Women everywhere are beginning to recognize the immense value of sisterhood once again. We're learning that we can't possibly get everything we need from one other person or by standing alone. Instead, we need a community—a network of support that allows us to thrive collectively.

I've seen this shift in my own life. After my divorce, I felt a profound sense of isolation despite being surrounded by people every day. I longed for deeper connections with other women who shared my values and aspirations. So, I decided to join a wine group. We met at a couple's home, and before long, it was a group of 20-30 people who regularly got together over food, wine, and life. That was many years ago now, and while we now live in different states, my dear friend Lisa, the founder of that group, is still someone I look forward to catching up with over a glass of wine whenever I am in California.

Over the years, several women in that group have cheered each other on through career changes, personal struggles, and triumphs. This sisterhood is a source of strength and joy I can depend on.

We Are Built for Connection

Our biology and psychology are wired for connection. Studies have shown that social support is crucial for our mental and physical health. For women, in particular, these bonds can reduce stress, improve well-being, and even increase longevity.

In many ways, we're returning to our roots. Women's circles, networking groups, and online communities dedicated to supporting and empowering women are flourishing. We're redefining what it means to connect in the modern world, leveraging technology to bridge gaps rather than widen them.

An Invitation to Start or Join Something

I invite you to consider how you might cultivate or deepen your own sisterhood.

- Start Something: Is there a group or gathering you've been yearning for but haven't found? Perhaps it's a local meet-up around a shared interest, a virtual discussion group, or a collaborative project. Take the initiative to bring it to life. Chances are, others are seeking the same connection.

- Join Something: Seek out existing communities that resonate with you. Whether it's a professional network, a hobbyist club, or a support group, immersing yourself in a community can enrich your life in unexpected ways.

If you're looking for a place to connect, share, and grow, I'd love for you to join us at BraveGreatness.com. It's a Substack space where we can come together to read, chat, and uplift one another. You're welcome to hang out and be part of our growing sisterhood.

Self-Reflection Exercise: Finding or Creating Your Sisterhood

Let's take a moment to reflect on your current connections and how you might expand or deepen them.

1. Assess Your Current Connections

- Do you feel isolated or lacking in meaningful connections with other women?

- Are there people in your life you'd like to get to know better or reconnect with?

2. Identify Your Interests and Values

- What activities, causes, or topics are you passionate about?

- How might these interests guide you toward like-minded individuals?

3. Explore Opportunities

- Research local groups, clubs, or organizations that align with your interests.

- Look for online communities or forums where you can engage and connect.

4. Take Action

- Reach out to someone you'd like to know better.

- Attend a meeting or event, even if it feels a bit outside your comfort zone.

- Consider starting your own group or initiative, no matter how small.

5. Reflect on Your Experiences

- After engaging with others, take time to reflect on how it felt.

- What did you enjoy? What might you do differently next time?

Closing Thoughts

Creating a sisterhood isn't just about expanding your social circle—it's about building a network of support, inspiration, and empowerment. It's about recognizing that we're stronger together and that our collective wisdom and experiences enrich each of us.

As we reconnect with the age-old tradition of women's communities, we reclaim a part of ourselves that's been neglected in the hustle of modern life. We remember that collaboration trumps competition, that empathy fosters growth, and that together, we can achieve remarkable things.

So, I encourage you to take that step—reach out, connect, and embrace the sisterhood that's waiting for you.

In our next chapter, we'll delve into 'Habits.' We'll explore mindfulness practices to stay present, holistic self-care, simplifying routines, and aligning actions with your values—even when the activity isn't a 'Hell Yes,' but the why behind it is compelling.

Chapter 14

Habits

Have you ever noticed how the small things we do every day can add up to significant changes over time? Habits are the invisible architecture of our daily lives. They create the consistency we need to support our goals, help us be the adult in the room, ensure we get the right amount of sleep, and ultimately enable us to thrive.

Let's dive into the power of habits and how establishing purposeful routines can transform our lives. We'll start by exploring the foundation of a good day: the evening and morning routines.

The Evening Routine

I used to think the key to a productive morning was all about what I did after waking up. It took me longer than I'd like to admit to recognize that a successful morning begins the night before. To tackle the world each day, we need adequate rest; for most of us, that means about eight hours of sleep per night.

But here's a lesson I learned the hard way: it's not just about the number of hours you spend in bed—it's about the quality of that sleep and how you wind down before it.

Preparing for Rest

I used to crawl into bed at midnight, expecting to fall asleep instantly, only to find myself tossing and turning. It dawned on me that just like a car needs time to slow down before it stops, our minds need time to transition from the busyness of the day to the tranquility of sleep.

Now, I make it a point to get into bed at least an hour before I need to be asleep. This buffer allows me to unwind without feeling rushed. And here's a game-changer: I now keep screens out of the bedroom. Honestly, it's a new habit that I've put into place. No more scrolling through my phone or watching late-night TV.

Instead, I try to engage in calming activities:

- Reading: There's nothing like getting lost in a good book. It quiets the mind and prepares it for rest.

- Journaling: Reflecting on the day helps me process my thoughts and release lingering worries.

- Coloring or Crocheting: These simple, repetitive tasks are surprisingly soothing and require enough focus to distract from racing thoughts.

The Challenge of Consistency

One habit I've been working on is doing an extended meditation at least three to four nights a week. I have a guided meditation that's an hour long, and when I stick to it, the benefits are profound. It calms my mind, reduces stress, and improves my sleep quality and overall happiness.

But I'll be honest—it's a challenge. If I land in bed later than planned, I tend to skip it. I've had stretches where I'm consistent for months, and then one weeknight out throws off my schedule. It's a work in progress, and that's okay. Habits take time to solidify, and setbacks are part of the journey.

Setting Boundaries

I've learned that setting boundaries around these habits is crucial. For me, that means saying 'no' to weeknight outings. It wasn't an easy decision—I love socializing and didn't want to feel like I was missing out. However, I realized that sacrificing my sleep impacted not just that night but my entire week.

By prioritizing my evening routine, I'm investing in my well-being.

The Morning Routine

For years, I fought the idea of being a morning person. The allure of the snooze button is strong, and early mornings felt like a punishment. But over time, I discovered the magic that mornings hold when you embrace them intentionally.

Embracing Early Mornings

Now, I wake up at 5:45 a.m., and that first hour is sacred—it's all about me. This quiet time before the world wakes up has become my favorite part of the day.

Here's what my morning routine looks like:

- Physical Activity: I start with a workout. It doesn't have to be intense—even a 20-minute yoga session or a brisk walk gets the blood flowing and energizes me for the day.

- Journaling: After exercising, I sit down with my journal. I jot down my thoughts, set intentions for the day, and express gratitude. This practice centers me and aligns my mindset.

- Meditation: If time allows, I meditate for at least 10 minutes. It's a way to cultivate mindfulness and carry a sense of calm into the day ahead.

- Showering and Getting Ready: It's time to get ready for the day, feeling refreshed and grounded.

Look, I get it. If you're groaning at me, I respect that. It's taken me many attempts over the years to embrace it. I still want to hit that snooze button. But I know I'll be happier if I don't.

Greeting the Sun

One ritual that has made a significant difference is stepping out onto my balcony to greet the sun. There's something profoundly grounding about feeling the morning air and watching the sky awaken with light.

This simple act helps regulate my circadian rhythm—the internal clock that tells our bodies when to sleep and wake. Exposure to natural light in the morning boosts mood, reduces stress, and can help you fall asleep more easily at night.

The Importance of Regulating Your Circadian Rhythm

Our bodies thrive on routine, and aligning our habits with our natural rhythms enhances our overall well-being.

- Improved Sleep Quality: Consistent sleep and wake times help regulate sleep cycles, leading to more restful sleep.

- Enhanced Mood: Exposure to morning light increases serotonin production, which improves mood and energy levels.

- Reduced Stress: Establishing routines reduces decision fatigue and creates a sense of stability.

Building a Foundation

These habits—the evening wind-down and the intentional morning—are my foundation. They're not about rigid schedules but creating a supportive framework that nurtures my physical, mental, and emotional health.

I'm always working on incorporating new habits and simplifying my routines. For example, I'm experimenting with meal prepping on Sundays to make healthy eating easier during the week. I'm also exploring new forms of exercise to keep things interesting.

Aligning Habits with Your Values

In Chapter 11, we talked about defining our personal values. Aligning our habits with these values ensures that our daily actions reflect what's truly important to us.

For me, valuing health and well-being means prioritizing sleep, exercise, and mindfulness. Valuing personal growth translates into journaling and reading. Connecting habits to values makes them more meaningful and easier to maintain.

Reflecting on Your Habits

Take a moment to consider:

- Do your daily habits support your values and goals?

- Do they help you show up as the person you want to be?

- Are there habits you want to cultivate or let go of to better align with your values?

Self-Reflection Exercise: Designing Your Supportive Habits

Let's work through an exercise to identify and establish habits that align with your values.

Step 1: Identify Your Core Values

- Review Your Values: Refer back to the values you defined in Chapter 11.

- Prioritize: Choose three to five core values that are most important to you right now.

Step 2: Assess Your Current Habits

- List Your Habits: Write down your current daily habits in the morning and evening.

- Evaluate Alignment: For each habit, ask yourself:

- Does this habit support or hinder my core values?

- How does it impact my well-being and goals?

Step 3: Identify Habits to Cultivate

- Choose Supportive Habits: Based on your values, identify habits you want to establish or strengthen.

- Be Specific: Define what the habit looks like. For example, "Meditate for 10 minutes each morning" or "Read for 30 minutes before bed."

Step 4: Plan for Implementation

- Set Realistic Goals: Start small to build momentum. Committing to a manageable habit is better than setting yourself up for overwhelm.

- Create a Routine: Decide when and how you'll incorporate the new habit into your day.

- Prepare for Obstacles: Anticipate challenges and plan strategies to overcome them. For instance, if you're tempted to check your phone before bed, consider charging it in another room.

Step 5: Establish Boundaries

- Protect Your Time: Set boundaries that support your habits, such as declining late-night invitations or setting "do not disturb" hours.

- Communicate Needs: Let those around you know about your new routines so they can support you.

Step 6: Reflect and Adjust

- Monitor Progress: Keep track of your habits and note how they make you feel.

- Be Flexible: If something isn't working, adjust as needed. Habits should serve you, not the other way around.

Closing Thoughts

Building and maintaining habits is an ongoing journey. It's not about perfection but about progress and consistency. There will be days when things don't go as planned, and that's okay. What's important is returning to your intentions and continuing forward.

Remember, habits are powerful tools that can transform your life in meaningful ways when aligned with your values. They provide the structure that allows you to thrive, helping you become the person you aspire to be.

As we wrap up this chapter, I encourage you to take the time to design habits that support your unique path. Celebrate your efforts, be patient with yourself, and embrace the positive changes that unfold.

In our conclusion, we'll explore The Joy of Missing Out (JOMO). We'll delve into the happiness found in choosing your experiences, accepting and loving yourself as you are, and navigating triggers and guilt with self-regulation and resilience. I look forward to sharing this closing journey with you.

Conclusion

The Joy of Missing Out

I used to feel compelled to be in every room, attend every event, and seize every opportunity that came my way—the thought of missing out on something amazing gnawed at me. As I got older, that need morphed into a sense of obligation—I felt like I was letting people down if I didn't show up to everything I was invited to. The fear of missing out wasn't just about the experiences anymore but about disappointing others.

But then something shifted. I began to realize there's true joy in choosing my own experiences. Why should others dictate where I live, how I live, or what I do for fun? One day, I stumbled upon a term that perfectly encapsulated this revelation: JOMO—the Joy of Missing Out. It resonated deeply with me. Embracing JOMO meant I could find happiness in the choices I made for myself without the pressure of external expectations.

Choosing My Experience

A true story that illustrates this is my relationship with social media. I haven't posted on Facebook since last January, and honestly, I have no desire to return to it. For me, this is the embodiment of the Joy of Missing Out. I don't miss the endless scrolling, the barrage of 'opportunities,' or the unsolicited messages about products and events I have no interest in.

That's not to say I don't value the connections I made there or the friends who shared snippets of their lives. But I realized that my time and energy are precious. By stepping away from a few platforms that weren't enriching my life, I opened up space for activities and relationships that truly matter to me. My businesses run just fine without *every one* of those spaces, and I'm happier without the time spent in them.

This decision isn't about withdrawing from the world; it's about being selective about who gets my attention and where I invest my energy. And let me tell you, it's been one of the best decisions I've made in years. I feel joy in choosing my experience and in curating a life that reflects my values and desires.

Accepting and Loving Yourself Just As You Are

I know I mentioned this a bit already, but I grappled with insecurities when I first started writing this book. I worried about coming across as someone who has it all figured out—like some wannabe guru with perfect habits and flawless relationships. That isn't who I am at all. I am entirely, wholly human and every chapter in this book is about a journey I am still on. In fact, I don't think this journey ever ends—we just move on to different aspects of it.

I stumble and make mistakes all the time. Really. I hope these pages have conveyed that I'm just as imperfect as anyone else. My goal was never to present a 'be like me' narrative. Instead, I wanted to share the insights and lessons I've gathered over the past decade for your consideration. My eternal hope is that you'll take what resonates with you and leave what doesn't.

I'm still working on accepting and loving myself just as I am. It's a journey, not a destination. What I want more than anything is for you to see that if I can navigate these challenges, you can, too. If I can learn to start embracing myself with all my imperfections, you can also.

Navigating Triggers and Guilt

Triggers and guilt will come—they always do. Life has a way of presenting us with situations that stir up old wounds or insecurities. Over time, I've learned the importance of establishing a response to triggers when they happen.

If I'm alone, I have a practice that helps me re-center:

- Deep Breathing: I place my hands over my heart and take slow, intentional breaths.

- Visualization: I close my eyes and envision myself evolving, moving from where I was to where I am now.

- Affirmation: I remind myself that growth is a continuous process, and it's okay to be a work in progress.

When I'm in public, the process is more discreet but just as effective:

- Inner Dialogue: I take a deep breath and tell myself, "You've got this."

- Grounding: I focus on the sensations around me—the feeling of my feet on the ground, the ambient sounds—to stay present.

The guilt or shame spiral can be torturous. In those moments, I remind myself to be the adult in the room. I question the stories my inner critic—my Harley—tells me. Are these thoughts based on reality or distortions rooted in past experiences?

An Invitation to Give Yourself Grace

Here's my invitation to you: Give yourself some grace. Extend to yourself the kindness and understanding you would offer a dear friend. Much like Harley, your inner self may have been through a lot and might get confused or stuck at times. It's your compassionate guidance that will see her through those moments.

Remember, self-compassion isn't about letting yourself off the hook for mistakes; it's about recognizing that imperfection is part of the human experience. It's about acknowledging your struggles without judgment and committing to treating yourself with patience and care.

Thank You for Sharing This Journey

As we conclude this journey together, thank you for allowing me to share my stories and reflections. Writing this book has been an exercise in vulnerability and authenticity. I hope that in these pages, you've found insights that resonate with you, challenges that inspire you, and perhaps a sense of camaraderie in knowing that none of us have it all figured out.

Life is a beautiful, messy adventure filled with highs and lows. Embracing the Joy of Missing Out, accepting ourselves as we are, and navigating challenges with grace are all part of creating a fulfilling and authentic life.

Moving Forward

As you move forward, I encourage you to:

- Choose Your Own Experience: Live life on your terms. Embrace the activities, relationships, and goals that align with your true self.

- Practice Self-Compassion: Be gentle with yourself. Celebrate your progress and forgive your missteps.

- Stay Present: Engage fully in the moments that make up your life. Savor them.

- Connect with Others: Seek out communities and relationships that support and uplift you.

Remember, you are not alone on this journey. We're all navigating our own paths, learning and growing along the way.

With gratitude and warmth,
Charlie

ABOUT THE AUTHOR

CHARLIE McCLAIN is a respected thought leader and private executive coach. She specializes in guiding dynamic women through the challenges of Driven Woman Syndrome to become unapologetic, visionary leaders. As a certified life coach with a master's in psychology, she delves into leadership and the complexities of the self-discovery process. Her current weekly articles on Substack cover all aspects of 'the work' related to a woman's well-being.

Charlie's work supports and challenges driven women to approach all aspects of personal development work as 'self-integration work,' embracing the whole self rather than the usual fragmented approach.

As a driven woman who went from being an educator and business owner, living a millionaire lifestyle—to arriving homeless in a shelter for battered women—then courageously rebuilding her life as a professional and entrepreneur, Charlie brings her unique experiences to her work. Through a wide array of techniques and practices she calls Inner Alchemy™, Charlie helps her clients explore transformation from the inside out, challenge the expectations and stressors of modern-day living, and redefine success on their own terms.

With two decades of experience and a Master's in Education, she began a series of research projects on the subconscious, beliefs, and meditation. As Charlie pursued her second Master's degree in Psychology, she focused her research on habits she dubbed Driven Woman Syndrome. This work, her inspirational experiences, and her use of digestible analogies are the bedrock of Charlie's programs, talks, and workshops.

Charlie is an international speaker, best-selling contributing author, executive contributor for Brainz Magazine, a two-time Crea Global Award recipient, and has been featured in USA Today, Fox, NBC, and more.

You can find Charlie through her site, writercharliemcclain.com

www.ingramcontent.com/pod-product-compliance
Lightning Source LLC
Chambersburg PA
CBHW072152090426
42740CB00012B/2238